REMEMBERING
A CHAMPION

RALPH HENDERSON SCOTT

REMEMBERING

A

CHAMPION

By
Gayle Lane Fitzgerald

Typesetting by Photoset, Inc., Raleigh, N.C.

Printed by Edwards & Broughton Co., Raleigh, N.C.

For a lifetime of dedicated public service to the people of Alamance County and North Carolina, and especially for being a champion of those who have no champion — the handicapped, the needy and the disadvantaged, this evidence of our esteem and appreciation is hereby presented with our love and affection.

Inscription written by D.J. Walker, Jr.
for plaque presented to Ralph Scott
by Senior Opportunities and Services
   of Alamance County
May 11, 1981

ACKNOWLEDGMENTS

The family of Ralph Scott and the author wish to acknowledge the many people who have shared their time and their memories for this book. We are deeply grateful to Ruth Albright, Jack Aulis, Rev. Ralph Buchanan, Dr. Harrie Chamberlin, Russell Clay, Weldon Denny, Joel Fleishman, Bill Friday, Jim Graham, Monk Harrington, Betsy Warren Harrison, Melvin Hearn, Jim Hunt, Nell Isley, Jim Keene, Rudolf and Katrina Kronbergs, Otis Lackey, Tom Lambeth, Dr. Sarah Morrow, Reid Poovey, Anne Queen, Sam Ragan, Marshall Rauch, Ruth Relos, Stilsie Reynolds, Dr. Bill Roberts, Senator Terry Sanford, Bob and Jessie Rae Scott, Dr. Donald Stedman, Sheriff John Stockard, D.J. Walker, Jr., Lindsay Warren, Jr., and Tom White. Without their kind generosity of time and love, this book would not have been possible.

TABLE OF CONTENTS

FOREWORD

Ralph Scott is a rare man. During a long, multi-faceted career, he founded and was president of a highly successful company and became a state politician of legendary stature. His life has been one of great and lasting achievements, monuments to his energy and wisdom and concern for the citizens of his native North Carolina.

But the monuments tell only part of the story. Equally significant has been Ralph Scott's impact on individuals. For those who have known him, he has also been a teacher, showing them the meaning of loyalty, the strength of compassion, and the force of Christianity in action. They will always remember him as a champion of values as well as causes. They will remember him as a man who taught with tenderness and fought with wit and achieved greatness with humility. His legacy to them is not only the monuments of achievement but the memories of a unique man whose humor and vision and love enriched their lives.

This book is a collection of those memories.

I

THE MAKING OF A CHAMPION

The New York Times for Saturday, December 12, 1903, printed the weather forecast at the top of the first page. It said, "Fair, south winds, shifting to the east."

There was indeed a south wind that day, blowing into the little community of Hawfields, North Carolina. It was a warming wind, a strong wind, a wind that would later sweep through the state to comfort and heal and nurture the land and its people, a wind named Ralph Henderson Scott.

Ralph was born that day to a family whose roots had been planted there along the banks of the Haw River in the 1700s. His ancestors helped to settle the community, and the family torch of public service that was lit by the first sheriff of the county passed from one generation to the next down to Ralph.

Ralph's father, Robert Walter Scott, was a farmer and statesman and, in many ways, to know the father is to know the son. After the elder Scott died in 1929, he continued to live in the vibrant memories of his neighbors and colleagues. Lifelong family friend Lexie Ray talked about those memories at a gathering in 1981 to honor the Scotts. He said:

WHEN HISTORIANS RECORD 20th century North Carolina, the name "Scott" will be in large print, as no record of this century can be written without a prominent portion devoted to their contributions, participation, and bold leadership. For 80 years, "Farmer Bob" Scott [Ralph's father] and his descendants have played a major role in every worthwhile movement affecting our people.

I'm probably one of only a few persons in this audience that enjoyed the good fortune of having known Mr. Bob Scott. I remember how he looked, how he walked, and especially how he was known as a master farmer and helped lead agricultural and educational progress in our community and state. He and my daddy were neighbors and great friends. He kept fine cattle, guineas, goats, sheep, hogs, chickens, and sorry looking mules. Mr. Bob served his community and state in many capacities. He was a member of the State Board of Agriculture [under six governors], served in the N.C. Senate and House of Representatives, and was a member of the Board of Trustees at N.C. State College [later renamed N.C. State University]. So the Scotts you have known and know had some real "branch head" beginnings. Their qualities of leadership were literally bred in them. This was a large family including medical doctors, farmers, educators, county commissioners, senators, and governors.

At that same dinner in 1981, Moore County legislator Clyde Auman also remembered Ralph's family and the legacy that was left to him, his brother Kerr, and Kerr's son Robert:

THE STATE OF MASSACHUSETTS has had its Kennedys and its jetset glamor. Virginia has had its Byrds. Further to the south have been the Longs of Louisiana, and the Talmadges of Georgia. North Carolina has been more fortunate. We have had the Scotts who have, without a question, contributed more than any other family to the progress of our state and the advancements of its people. Tonight, we celebrate a century of service to North Carolina by the Scotts. It was in the fall of 1881 that Robert Walter Scott . . . better known as Farmer Bob went north at the age of 20 to learn new farming methods in Pennsylvania and New York. Not long afterwards, he was married and became a deacon and later an elder in the Hawfields Presbyterian Church. He became a leader in the Farmer's Alliance, elected to the legislature at the age of 27, supported the establishment of . . . North Carolina State [University] — he and Cameron Morrison were the whips who got Governor Aycock's education program through the General Assembly. From this brief and incomplete sketch of Farmer Bob, we can see some of the traits that have been passed down from one generation to the next. His trip north reflected a desire to learn, an openness to new ideas, an attitude of welcome change rather than fearing it. . . .

It was in Farmer Bob's tradition that Kerr, Ralph, and Robert each became active in the Hawfields Church, in public service, and in farm groups; so active that the name Scott has become synonymous with dairying, Democrats, politics and Presbyterians, good roads, Ben Roney and the Grange, with education and elections, with boldness and branch head boys, with humor, courage, and cash management.

Woodrow Price, former managing editor of *The News and Observer* said simply that the Scotts were "the smartest country boy family North Carolina has ever produced."

In 1952, the new poultry and research center at North Carolina State University was dedicated to Farmer Bob and the building was named Scott Hall in his memory. The money for the new facility came as a result of Ralph's leadership in the state legislature. At the dedication ceremony, Farmer Bob's old friend and colleague, Clarence Poe, editor of *The Progressive Farmer*, talked about some of his dreams:

ROBERT WALTER SCOTT was not only a good farmer, but he wished to see the whole South become a land of fertile soils, enterprising "live-at-home" farmers, fine livestock, and happy country homes. . . . [He] devoted a lifetime to working constantly for this realization. . . . [He was a man of] vision, vim, and versatility . . . one of the most successful men that North Carolina has yet produced.

Ralph's mother, Elizabeth Hughes Scott, was a great match for Farmer Bob. She shared his strong values of faith and honor and his deep love of the land. With a keen business mind and energetic enthusiasm, she successfully managed the family farm while her husband was involved in other activities. She also cared for their children and home and wrote witty articles for *The Progressive Farmer*, telling other farm wives how to make their homes more attractive.

Ralph was one of fourteen children, although three of them died in infancy. The siblings closest to him in age were also close to him in character. His brother Kerr, who was seven years older, grew up to become North Carolina's Commissioner of Agriculture, governor, and U.S. senator. His sister Elizabeth Carrington, just a year older, was a leading force in health education in the state and was instrumental in the founding of the School of Nursing at the University of North Carolina in Chapel Hill. That school's building, Carrington Hall, is named for her.

All the Scott children were raised with a clear understanding of what was important in life: the church, a good education, and public service. As Ralph later said, "All the Scotts are kind of individualists." But their individualism and fierce defense of their own convictions never overshadowed their sense of Christian love, family loyalty, and commitment to helping those in need.

In 1914, Ralph's mother died. His father later married Miss Ella Anderson who was a school teacher. Ralph often spoke of her, saying he couldn't have had a better step-mother.

The man that Ralph Henderson Scott became was the result not only of his parents and their parents and grand-parents, but of the life he knew on his family's farm nestled in that little Haw River community. It was a life in which he labored side by side with black field hands and ate with them at their homes. It was a life in which, even as a boy, he got up early and worked hard and thought nothing of shooing flies out of the molasses before he ate it on his lunchtime biscuit.

In that close-knit community, he learned the interdependence of neighbors. He saw others, especially his parents, sharing all they had with those in need. He grew up believing in the basic goodness of people and in the responsibility of individuals toward one another.

Ralph's large family became even larger when teachers from the community school boarded there. He once said that he learned young how to get along with people because there were so many of them to get along with in his home.

Longtime friend and colleague Melvin Hearn says that those early years, on that farm, in that home, and in that community, had a profound effect on Ralph:

COMPASSION WAS WOVEN into him as a child and he grew up with a deep sensitivity for those who were weaker. Two incidents in particular helped to shape his character.

One of those incidents was a local election to establish a high school in Hawfields. A new school meant new taxes, so there was considerable opposition. Emotions grew hot and the only black man who was literate and therefore qualified to vote was threatened with the loss of his job if he supported the proposed school. Nevertheless he did, and on election day, the proposal passed by one vote.

Throughout his life, Ralph would continue to hear in his mind the church bells that rang in Hawfields that day, a day when education triumphed in a community because of one vote by one courageous black farmhand.

The other incident also occurred when Ralph was very young. Melvin Hearn says that it was a turning point in the development of his great compassion for others. Ralph was out in the field one day when the sheriff came to arrest one of the black men who worked on the farm. Ralph never forgot the fear he felt at that moment, as he watched someone he knew and liked being taken away at gunpoint. He ran to a black neighbor to ask why such a thing had happened. And he never forgot the reply: "Boy, you don't never argue with the man who has the gun." The boy refused to accept that, and he grew up to argue fearlessly with many people who held guns of power or wealth or influence against those who were powerless and poor and alone.

Melvin Hearn remembers other stories that Ralph would tell about his childhood, stories of tranquility and joy and humor. He would talk about the jobs that each child had on the farm and about his delight when he moved up from kitchen duties to barn chores. This, he thought, was the key to his future. He loved the cows, loved milking them, and would gleefully aim a random squirt or two at the flies that hovered about him. Undoubtedly, Meville

Dairy which Ralph later founded had its beginnings here, on a wooden stool in Farmer Bob's barn.

Hearn remembers Ralph talking about the black youngsters with whom he played. He often went to their homes to eat and he would talk about the comradeship and equality of those good times. There was one black family in particular who lived nearby. Ralph said that when he was small, he and his sister Elizabeth often played with the two children in the family. They called one of the children "Sister." Ralph said that he probably ate as many meals at their home as he did at his own, meals that usually featured cornbread and molasses.

Ralph talked about the meals at his own home too. Because there were so many people, both family and boarders, the younger children sat at a side table. Ralph always claimed that was the reason for his good health — being raised at the side table where there was less rich food.

It was a life without pretense, a life in which all individuals were of equal value, a life in which joys and sorrows were shared and each experience strengthened the bonds that tied Ralph to his roots and to his fellowman.

Newspaperman Jack Aulis says the character of the Hawfields community has had a tremendous influence on the Scott family:

> ALL THE SCOTTS are like that. They really identify with that place and that land. It's one of their strongest attributes.

Russell Clay, another longtime friend and colleague, wrote this:

THERE ARE THOSE who seem to think that they owe nothing to the past or to their forebears. Ralph Scott was not one of these. He felt he owed everything to those who preceded him and helped shape his life in some way. . . . [He often talked] about those men and women of old who settled this community, who developed it, who brought education and health care and jobs and opportunity to the people. . . . He referred to his parents and his parents' parents and their contemporaries throughout the neighborhood who worked to make the path just a little smoother for those who came after them.

Ralph was deeply affected by the character of the people he grew up with, by their plain talk and intense loyalty, by their devotion to honor and community service, by their belief in hard work and its reward of satisfaction. Most off all, he was shaped by the source of their strength: their abiding, unshakeable faith.

Ralph's formal education was somewhat scant in those early years. The school closed each year for the annual flu epidemic. In addition, Ralph was the only student in the Hawfields High School Class of 1921. So the school decided to graduate him with the Class of 1920. "They just went ahead and shoved me out," he later said. He had only had eighteen months of high school education.

Even so, those years in the community schools made a lasting impression on him. There was one teacher in particular whom he never forgot. Years later, when the walls of his office had become crowded with autographed pictures of North Carolina governors and U.S. presidents and world leaders, there was one picture that stood out among the rest. It was the photograph of a young woman with an inscription in Ralph's hand that said, "Miss Martha Holt, Graham, N.C., My favorite teacher at Hawfields, 1914, Ralph H. Scott."

From high school, Ralph went to North Carolina State University, the college that his father had helped start, to study agriculture. Jack Aulis later interviewed Ralph about those college years and wrote about them in his *News and Observer* column, Carolina Crossroads:

> SEN. SCOTT, I SAID, what exactly WAS the Ancient Order of the Yellow Cur?
>
> "It was just something you could get into if you couldn't get into anything else," he said. "It was a bunch of agriculture students. We'd get together once in awhile and sit around and talk. Couldn't do anything else. We didn't have any money to spend."
>
> . . . According to the college annual, he was called "Scotty" in those days, although he never has been called that before or since. He was president of the Leazer Literary Society, a debating society, and was class vice president his senior year. But his future, the annual said, was not politics. It was to be "track coach of the Haw River college of women."
>
> Scott was, you see, a track star, the captain and chief asset of N.C. State's state champion cross-

country team. And he also ran the mile (4:30) and the two miles.

I said I had been told the cross-country team was the only winning athletic team State College had in 1924. "I believe it was," Scott said. I had, in fact, heard that State's basketball team . . . had lost to Durham High. "I didn't think it was that bad," he said, "but it was bad."

The main problems Scott had at State, he said, were physics and chemistry. They gave him a fit. "That was partly because I only ever had about 18 months of high school."

. . . "My brother Kerr, he was on the track team out there at State, too (1917)," Scott said. "He was a distance runner."

Is that why Ralph Scott went out for track — because his older brother had?

"Naw," the senator said. "All the Scotts kill themselves eatin'. I heard you got better food if you got to the training table. That was the only reason I went out."

His college annual in 1924 had this to say about Ralph, after listing the names of 14 clubs and campus organizations of which he was a member or officer:

THIS SPECIMEN HAILS from the vicinity of Haw River, which he vows is the garden spot of the universe. On any other subject, he is a congenial enough soul, so we are willing to overlook his weakness of this one subject. Though not a "social guy" in the commonly accepted sense of the word, he slips away now and then to Mebane; and the whisper goes around that something in the left side of his chest goes "pit-pat" whenever a certain name is mentioned. We do not go so far as to say that he is actually in love, but we do wonder what else could draw him within hailing distance of Mebane.

"Scotty" is quite an accomplished performer on the cinder path, having won the State championship in cross-country and being one of the best distance men in these parts. He is also a wide awake and influential man on the campus; we have no fear for his future after he leaves college.

The "certain name" that made his heart beat faster was Hazeleene Tate. She was, Ralph later said, "the only woman I ever really went with." He never forgot the day they met and he often recalled it to his friend and colleague Ruth Relos:

HE SAID THAT THE FIRST TIME he laid eyes on his wife, she had on a pink sweater. He said, "I had just gotten done milking cows and I had gunk all over my shoes. She came by with two other girls and she was so pretty and pink. We became sweethearts in high school. And when I left to go to college, people kept saying, 'Don't you want to go out with this girl or that over at Meredith or Peace or St. Mary's?' And I'd say, 'No, I have a sweetheart at home.'"

She was his first and only love.

On November 11, 1925, she and Ralph were married. She became his partner in all that he did, helping him in his business, supporting him and sacrificing for him that he might achieve his goals, providing him with the security of a loving home, raising their three children, Miriam Tate, Ralph Henderson Jr., and William Clevenger.

In 1927 Ralph took a step which he believed would set the course of his life. He created Melville Dairy. The business thrived, becoming one of the leading dairies in the state. On the occasion of the dairy's 25th anniversary, its history was recorded in a scrapbook:

BACK IN THE TWENTIES, young Ralph H. Scott, an Alamance County farm boy, with a brand-new diploma from N.C. State College's School of Agriculture, had his sights set upon a market for the production of milk in Alamance County.

In the need of a little backing, he obtained his first loan from Charles A. Scott, president of The National Bank of Alamance in nearby Graham. In March 1927, he and his brother Henry, with Jim Gibson and Sam Patton, began the construction of a milk barn, with a bottle sterilizing room, on Henry's farm located in the Hawfields Community.

Electricity was not yet available to rural areas and concentrated cement mixers and other modern-day building materials and carpentry tools were unheard of. As Jim Gibson recalls, "The only tools we had were a hammer and a saw piece — it was undoubtedly the hard way to build a barn, but we didn't know it then." An unexpected snow — a deep one — completely covering the foundation, delayed construction for awhile; however, the structure was completed and on August 1, Melville's first milk — three or four gallons — was bottled. . . .

The first day's sale amounted to $1.95; total sales for first month's operation, $167.81.

Ralph Scott, the one and only routeman, drove the Model-A Ford truck exactly 966 miles in making the first month's deliveries. Henry Scott was the sole producer with a herd of registered Jerseys. Mrs. Ralph Scott, the dairy's first bookkeeper, took telephone orders at her home. . . .

Ralph, the routeman, delivered his milk seven days a week. The former cross-country champion would park his truck on North Main Street in Burlington and run all over the area with his deliveries in order to save wear and tear on the truck. He wasn't the only one working hard to make the new business a success. Ralph later said:

TO SAVE ON OTHER EXPENSES, Hazeleene used to run every roll of adding machine tape through the machine four times before throwing it away.

[I] never missed a day during my first six years operating Melville Dairy. . . . I had a cold or two, but we never missed delivery. I could run all day every day back in those days when we delivered seven days a week and never get tired, and we didn't have any paved streets like we have now. . . .

If the State could save money now like we did then, we could get by on a whole lot less.

Their hard work paid off and Melville Dairy began to grow. The company's 25th anniversary history goes on to say:

MELVILLE SOON BEGAN BUYING from neighborhood dairy farmers who were eager to find a local market for their milk. The customers' list increased. Retailing milk in nearby towns was the next expansion step. . . .

Within a few years business had outgrown the little farm milk house and on January 15, 1935, the dairy was moved into a newly-erected, modernly-equipped processing plant in Burlington. Today [1952], the 80 by 80 foot structure represents a half-million dollar investment. . . .

In February 1948, a branch office — Smith-Melville Dairies — was opened in Raleigh, where Melville also has a large distribution of its products. . . .

Soon after that opening, Ralph had an offer from Longmeadow Dairy in Durham to buy his new Smith-Melville facility and he accepted it. His Burlington operation continued to grow. Ralph became a leading businessman in the area, participating in many important civic affairs. He was, at one time or another, president of the Burlington Kiwanis Club, the Burlington Chamber of Commerce, and the Alamance County Tuberculosis Association. He was a Mason, an Elk, and a member of numerous other organizations. He became a trustee of Elon College and Memorial Hospital of Alamance, and he served on the boards of several large companies.

But the prosperity and public recognition did not change the man. He did build a fine new home for his family, but it was not in the city of Burlington, close to his big business and social activities. It was on the family farm in Hawfields, close to his roots and within walking distance of his church. And his presidential office at that half-million dollar plant remained all his life a tiny room barely big enough for his desk, an unpretentious, undecorated room that could be reached only by walking up a long flight of stairs.

In that cramped little office, he kept a church bulletin on the wall by his desk that said:

The Boss and the Leader

The boss drives his men; the leader coaches them.
The boss depends upon authority; the leader on
     goodwill.
The boss inspires fear; the leader inspires
     enthusiasm.
The boss says "I;" the leader says "We."
The boss assigns the tasks; the leader sets the pace.
The boss says "Get here on time;" the leader gets
     there ahead of time.
The boss fixes the blame for a breakdown; the
     leader fixes the breakdown.

Ralph H. Scott

The boss knows how it is done; the leader shows
    how it is done.
The boss makes work a drudgery; the leader makes
    work a game.
The boss says "Go;" the leader says "Let's go."

II

A CHAMPION OF THE CHURCH

The great writer Eudora Welty once said, "A place that ever was lived in is like a fire that never goes out." The little community of Hawfields was such a place to Ralph. It was a fire that burned within him from his earliest memory, blazing a path before him of public service, lighting the way down a road of faith and compassion.

Longtime friend Anne Queen says of Ralph:

HE DREW HIS STRENGTH from his family and from the community and from his love of the soil of Alamance County. And he drew his strength from the church.

The church, in Ralph's case, was built by the same fearless pioneers who built the community. Hawfields Presbyterian Church was organized in 1755 by those early Scotch-Irish settlers who had come to the Haw River to put down roots. The roots grew as strong as the people and the little church of Hawfields has a long, proud history as a progressive, dynamic body of deeply religious parishioners.

Ralph was a third generation elder in the Hawfields Presbyterian Church. He was also, at one time or another, a deacon, Sunday school teacher, member of numerous church committees, chairman of the board, member and moderator of the Orange Presbytery, and trustee of both the Orange Presbytery School at Glade Valley and the Presbytery Camp at New Hope.

But his leadership roles in the church tell only part of the story. Just as the church and all it stands for was the center of the Hawfields community life, it also became the center of Ralph's life. It was the force that guided all he did and he lived his faith, every moment, every day. There's a story about a minister who once asked his flock, "If you were put on trial for being a Christian, would there be enough evidence to convict you?" The evidence of Ralph's life of faith comes from hundreds of people who were touched by his Christian compassion and generosity and love.

Reverend Ralph Buchanan was the minister of Hawfields Presbyterian Church from 1949-1959. He and his wife became close friends of Ralph and Hazeleene. Reverend Buchanan says:

WHEN CHRIST CAME into the world, He chose for Himself the role of a servant, and judging from the life that Ralph has lived, he must have patterned his own after the same ideal. His life has been one of service dedicated to the betterment of mankind.

Ralph Scott has helped more people in more different ways that any person I have ever known.

I have even seen him weep over the misfortune of others and have known of his borrowing money to support a worthy cause when his own funds were not immediately available.

Ralph was a great churchman, always faithful in attendance and serving wherever needed. He felt that the church should be the center of the community, providing facilities for recreation and other community functions. He was always concerned about young people and wanted the church to provide recreational as well as other types of entertainment so that they would have no need to go to less desirable places. He encouraged them to go to college and helped several to do so.

Reverend Buchanan remembers Hazeleene in much the same way:

RALPH [AND] HIS DEVOTED WIFE "Miss Hazeleene" shared the same philosophy, ideals, and goals and mutually supported each other in their endeavors. [They] were always sensitive to the joys and sorrows of people in the community and [were] diligent in assisting wherever possible.

Among the other things [I] recall:
— the spirit of genuine hospitality in their home;
— his quiet, humble, unassuming attitude in the midst of many honors and successes;
— his kindness toward and respect for all human beings regardless of race, creed, or social status;
— his openness and honesty in all situations;

— his sense of humor and his folksy understanding
of humankind.

Ralph's life has been a great inspiration.

Because of his prominence in the church community,
Ralph was often called on to make speeches. Those remarks
illuminate a side of his character that many people never
saw, a side that pondered earnestly and envisioned clearly
the role of the church in our lives. The country humor was
always there, but it was tempered by the fervency of his
faith.

Speaking to the Piedmont Presbytery in Piedmont,
South Carolina in 1967, Ralph said in part:

I KNOW MANY OF YOU have heard the story of the
two brothers who fell out and refused to speak to
one another for 20 years. Finally, one of them
became seriously ill, and their minister prevailed
upon the other brother to visit the one on his
deathbed.

Well, Zeb walked into the sick room and spoke
to Zeke and they made up. Then, as Zeb prepared
to leave, he turned to his sick brother and said,
"But remember, Zeke, if you get well, this doesn't
mean a thing."

Sometimes, that's the way it is with a revival.
Once the emotional crisis that prompted it has
passed, our good resolutions tend to fade and we
are back where we started. . . .

Perhaps my faith is too simple, but I believe that
the role of the church in leading all of us to better,

calmer days is just as important as the delicate negotiations conducted by skilled diplomats and heads of state.

I say this because, until we reach moral solutions to the great and grave problems which confront the world, the most we can hope for will be a temporary, uneasy peace. Accomodations based on fire-power and bomb-muscle will not endure.

Lasting tranquility will be ours only when we reach the human conscience. And while the scientists are trying to conquer outer space, the churches are going to have to try to conquer man's inner space. . . .

Now I, for one, do not think the church can assume its rightful role by withdrawing from the secular world. . . . I don't think a church can be *of* this world and not *in* it. . . .

If a church is true to its trust, it must go to the people where they live and provide the understanding and the guidance they need. A church cannot stand on the sidelines, so to speak, and quarterback the action on the field.

This may startle you, but often in quiet moments during my life I have thought that the atheists and the agnostics should rally to the support of the church with almost as much enthusiasm as the true believers.

I say that for this reason: the church and its teachings, as much as the law and its precepts, stand between civilization and the return to the jungle. And I submit that the law of the jungle would damage the non-believers as much as it would the rest of us. . . .

One of the great appeals of Jesus Christ, one of the secrets to the tremendous appeal He exerted in the long ago and exerts still, is that He held out hope to the masses — to the underprivileged, the disenfranchised, the disinherited, the forgotten, the people hanging onto the edge of life.

The church will ignore His example at great risk. The people who are comfortable and well-fed in the pews on Sunday morning are the minority. The restless, poorly fed, yearning people constitute the vast majority. Neither we nor the church should ignore them. Indeed, if we believe what we read in the Bible or hear from the pulpit, they are our first responsibility. . . .

When we isolate ourselves from the poor, insulate ourselves from the wrongs being visited upon the helpless, we not only are forfeiting our claim to membership in a church congregation, we are abdicating our responsibilities as rational human beings and moving closer to that invisible line that separates us from the lower animals.

In 1971, on the occasion of the installation of a new minister at the First Presbyterian Church in Greensboro, Ralph said:

ANY MINISTER HAS MY sympathy and this goes double for a new one. Some of the oldtimers will be forever comparing him to previous pastors. The lawyers will be watching his delivery. The business-men will be watching his work with the budget. Doctors will be observing his bedside manner. And, if you are like the rest of us Presbyterians, at one time or another you'll bridle and squirm when one of his sermons steps on your toes.

This beginning with a new pastor is a good time to take inventory of your church. It has a great and solid heritage. It has material as well as spiritual wealth. Most importantly, it is wealthy in terms of human resources. The value of these assets is deter-mined by how fully they are used. I urge you to invest them in your faith. If you do, the dividends will flow not only to this church, but to this city, this county, the state, and the nation. . . .

In 1985, *The Chapel Hill Newspaper* printed an editorial on ministers in which some of Ralph's remarks on the subject were quoted:

IN JUST ABOUT EVERY congregation, one group will think it's moving too fast in one direction and another will think it's moving too slow. The thermostat is too high for some, too low for others. The theology is too old or too new. But as long as we church-goers mix a little common sense with a whole lot of tolerance, I submit that these differences actually are healthy for our churches, our cause, and our country.

Nobody gets anywhere by standing still. Motion always creates friction. Without a certain amount

of creative tension, any kind of organization — the
church included — will stagnate. . . . We are going
to have to examine our own attitudes, motivation,
and goals. I've known some church members
who acted as if they thought the church should
be shaped in their own image — and that, I submit,
is not only stupid vanity, it is sinful and a
sacrilege. . . .

Ralph's most widely remembered religious speech came
in 1971 when he was retiring as moderator of the Orange
Presbytery. It was the speech of a man whose life and
religion are one:

WHEN WE READ THAT church membership is declin-
ing, and that fewer of our young people are prepar-
ing for the ministry, our first reaction may be one
of perplexity. Why? we ask.

I will leave the high-flown explanations to the
sociologists and church historians. But, as one layman, I think some of the factors are pretty clear.
And, sad to say, I think that a sizeable share of the
blame rests with the lay members of our church. If
that is true, then a major responsibility for revers-
ing this trend also rests with the lay members. . . .

By our attitudes and our statements, we have
inhibited those of our ministers who felt obligated
to tell us the unpalatable truths. We have wanted
messages which made us feel comfortable and

would not upset our digestions. Often our explanation was that "preachers should stick to religion and not dabble in politics and outside issues."

I submit that is utter nonsense. If religion is any good, it is not confined to Sunday and it does not touch only one part of a person's experience. It cannot be compartmentalized and be effective. A vital religion surrounds a person like an envelope and never leaves him. It guides him while he has on his overalls as well as his Sunday suit. . . .

Considering what he has to put up with, it's often difficult for me to imagine why anyone in his right mind would want to be a minister. He knows he's going to be underpaid . . . damned as "liberal" or railed against as a "conservative." I can't support this with scripture, but I imagine that when Jesus drove the money-changers out of the temple, he was labeled as an opponent of business by the Chamber of Commerce of that day.

The minister knows, or soon discovers, that his members are going to make demands upon him that they themselves would not tolerate from others.

The list goes on and on. After looking it over, I conclude our ministers persist because of an extraordinary sense of commitment to the church and to the gospel. They are, in fact, responding to a higher "call" to duty.

We laymen are subject to a "call" also, though we may ignore it. Because a layman cannot preach or sing, that doesn't mean he cannot serve, or that his obligation to use whatever talents he has is any less. . . .

We need to spend less time trying to decide whether a minister is a "liberal" or a "conservative" and pay more attention to his sincerity and his integrity. If he has the guts to tell us an unpopular truth, we ought to have the guts to tolerate it.

I cannot remember a time in my life when more people seemed to be yearning so fervently for the creation of a climate of hope. In a period of chaos, they are grasping for something with a semblance of stability. They seek peace and order. They seek reassurance that not all of the verities of life are collapsing before their eyes. They want something to believe in.

What the people want, I believe, is precisely what a vigorous, enlightened church is in a position to provide. Whether the church will respond depends upon you and me.

In 1983, Hawfields pastor A.B. Plexico made a speech in which he summed up Ralph's faith. The occasion was a dinner in Ralph's honor:

AT THE CLOSE OF OUR WORSHIP, I sometimes share with the congregation this charge:

"Go out into the world in peace: have courage: hold on to what is good: return no person evil for evil: strengthen the faint-hearted: support the weak: help the suffering: honor all people: love and serve the Lord, rejoicing in the power of the Holy Spirit."

On a recent Sunday when I had used the charge, "Uncle Ralph" on his way out of the sanctuary said in typical "Ralph Scott" fashion, "That thing you said at the last was good. It needs to be said a lot." I was not surprised. I was not surprised, because over the past twelve years I have come to know and respect Senator Scott as one who not only listens to such a charge but — more importantly — he is one who takes the charge to heart and tries to practice it in his daily life. . . .

Another thing I admire about this man is his progressive attitude toward the future. "Uncle Ralph" has a strong appreciation for tradition and the past. He has time and time again reminded us of the richness of our heritage as the Hawfields community and church. He has encouraged us and supported us in the collection and preservation of symbols of that heritage. He appreciates the fact that the present is rooted in the past. Yet he understands with the writer of Hebrews that "Where there is no vision, the people perish." This understanding keeps him on the cutting edge of life. It has instilled in him a boldness that dares to reach out and give shape to tomorrow. . . .

If I were to try and paint a word picture of my feelings about Senator Ralph H. Scott, I could do no better, I think, than to quote the words of the ancient author of the first Psalm. His words are descriptive of the one whom we are here to honor this evening. They go like this:

"Blessed is the man that walketh not in the counsel of the ungodly, nor standeth in the way of sinners, nor sitteth in the seat of the scornful. But his delight is in the law of the Lord . . . . And he shall be like a tree planted by the rivers of water, that bringeth forth his fruit in his season; his leaf also shall not wither; and whatsoever he doeth shall prosper."

III

A Champion Goes
to the Capital

In 1948 Ralph came to a fork in the road and, in true Scott tradition, he chose the path of family loyalty. That choice changed his life forever, leading him away from his beloved Hawfields with its green pastures and gentle people to the frenzy and fracas of the General Assembly in the capital city of Raleigh.

1948 was the year in which his brother Kerr resigned as North Carolina's Commissioner of Agriculture to run for governor. It was a race against considerable odds. It pitted the Democratic party establishment, known as the "Shelby dynasty" of former Governor O. Max Gardner, against another group within the party, known as the "branch head boys." That label, worn proudly by Kerr and his supporters, referred to people with rural roots, specifically, the folks who lived in remote country areas at the head of a branch.

Ralph said that branch head boys meant people "who lived on the dirt roads, who had no telephone service and no electric lights." Kerr understood those people and cared about them, and they knew it. They rallied behind him in greater numbers than anyone expected, and so a branch head boy moved into the Governor's Mansion.

The voters that year did not, however, send many branch head boys to the General Assembly. Kerr was unique, a man of the people whom the people trusted. Ralph later compared Kerr's situation to a Republican governor trying to work with a Democratic legislature, so hostile was the atmosphere in Raleigh against him. There was only one choice for Ralph. "I wanted to go down there and help Kerr out," Ralph said. "That's all I had in mind."

Ralph was a county commissioner at the time, the only elective office he had ever held. He decided to run for the State Senate and won. When the General Assembly convened in 1951, Ralph went to Raleigh and moved in temporarily with his brother at the Governor's Mansion. "That is when my education began," he said later. He watched and he learned about what he called "the disease of politics."

He learned well and became a significant asset to his brother. Kerr eventually won legislative support for his "Go Forward" program. As a result, there were record-breaking appropriations during his administration for capital improvements to state agencies and institutions; bonds were issued to pave nearly 15,000 miles of North Carolina roads (more than had been paved in the entire history of the state to that time); shipping facilities were built at the ports of Wilmington and Morehead City; and public utilities expanded electrical and telephone service to rural areas of the state. In addition, health facilities across the state were improved and more new hospitals were built during Kerr's administration than in any previous four-year period. Kerr's personal popularity and signficant achievements carried him to Washington. In 1954 he was elected to the U.S. Senate and, in that election, he received the largest majority ever given to a North Carolina Democratic senatorial candidate.

Education also got a share of the "Go Forward" program. Dr. Bill Roberts was professor of the Dairy Department at N.C. State during those years. He recalls:

WHEN KERR WAS GOVERNOR, there was a meeting between him, Ralph, the chancellor of N.C. State, and some people from the dairy industry. We met in an office building in downtown Raleigh. It was right after the war and everything was tight and the chancellor had not been able to get any money from the legislature. He told the governor at that meeting, "Governor, I'm at my wit's end. I have tried everything that I know and I can't get any support at all."

Now Ralph was always the one behind the scenes working on things and I don't think he got near the credit he deserves. Ralph was the one who got this meeting together. When the chancellor was through talking, Kerr said, "Well, how much do you need?"

"$11 million," said the chancellor.

Kerr turned to Ralph and said, "Well, let him have the money."

The money was appropriated. Scott Hall which was named after Kerr's and Ralph's father, Kilgore Hall, the facilities for poultry and forestry and the biological sciences — all those were built with the money that Kerr allocated and Ralph got appropriated by the legislature.

Ralph became well-known in Raleigh for his plain-spoken bluntness and absolute trustworthiness which earned him the respect of supporters and opponents alike. He also became famous for his wit.

Ralph and Kerr did not always agree — each had the Scott traits of intense independence as well as loyalty. One of their less serious disagreements arose over a state-owned boat that was docked on the North Carolina coast. The boat was frequently used by Democratic party officials for fishing trips. On one occasion, Ralph said he'd like to use the boat. Kerr said no, to which Ralph replied, "Kerr, as hard as we worked to win this election, as soon as we get to the trough, you cut off the slop."

Jim Graham and Melvin Hearn remember a story which illustrates the famous Scott loyalty:

WHEN KERR RAN FOR GOVERNOR in 1948, his headquarters were at the Carolina Hotel in Raleigh. A few days before the second Democratic primary, Kerr's campaign manager, Capus Waynick, called Ralph. Waynick said he felt that Kerr was going to win but he really needed another $10,000 to ensure a victory. He said that after Kerr won, he could easily get that amount of money and he asked if Ralph would guarantee it, which meant Ralph would have to pay it to the campaign should Kerr lose. Ralph replied that he had put all the money he could in Kerr's race, but he would think about it.

Ralph then called his brother, Dr. Floyd Scott, and told him the situation. Floyd's initial reaction was the same as Ralph's. But then Ralph said, "I sure would hate to wake up Sunday morning [the day after the election] and find Kerr had lost by just a few hundred votes because we wouldn't put up another $10,000." So Floyd said, "Well, go ahead and do it and I'll help guarantee the money."

That Sunday morning as Kerr and Ralph were walking to church, Ralph said, "Floyd told me to tell you that he's more glad than you are that you won because now we don't have to pay off that $10,000!"

The press enjoyed covering the two brothers, especially on issues where they disagreed and their fierce independence poked through. Ralph loved to tell the story of a reporter who cornered him one Monday and said that he had heard Ralph cussed Kerr in church the day before. Ralph told the reporter that was a lie — he said, "I cussed him *outside* of church."

As the years passed, Ralph's natural humor as well as his strength of character and deep compassion earned him a position as one of the most influential legislators in the state. He became chairman of the Finance and Appropriations Committees, a member and later chairman of the powerful Advisory Budget Commission, and a member of numerous other important legislative committees. A reporter once said that he had the face of "a benign bulldog" and others wrote about "his gravel voice" and "gruff manner." But beneath each comment was profound respect and admiration for this man who stood his ground and kept his word and cared about all the small and weak and helpless people, a man who worried about whether or not folks had jobs and what would happen to them when they were old and ill and handicapped, a man who worried about their children's education and health. Ralph continually turned those concerns into action, providing leadership and support for countless pieces of legislation to make life better for others.

He championed causes, not from a pedestal, but on the ground, shoulder to shoulder and hand in hand with those he sought to help. He had little use for people who placed themselves above the crowd. "Don't get your head too high," he'd say, "'cause someone's always gonna knock it off."

He fought for the rights of others without any sense of martyrdom. He wore no sackcloth into battle but instead a mantel of wit and wisdom. He knew the moment in a heated situation when tension strained the elastic issue to the point of snapping, and he would always relieve the moment with something quotable.

Like the time he suddenly stood up in the Senate in the midst of an exhausting debate and asked for the floor, whereupon he said, "I'd just like to observe that President Nixon has been in office ten days now and the sun hasn't shone since."

Or the moment during a lengthy committee hearing when the testimony had concluded and he rose and said,

"Now that we've heard from the intelligentsia, I wanna speak for my element."

Or his comment to a reporter who wanted to pull him out of an Appropriations Committee meeting: "I can't leave right now. It's throat-cutting time!"

Or the day when a group of teachers came to lobby the legislators. One of the young women stepped out of the group to speak to him privately. Recognizing her as a longtime family friend, he said in a voice that commanded the attention of everyone in the room, "Caroline, what are you doing here? They told me this was a militant group. You ain't even old enough to cuss yet."

He had no patience with anything less than the truth and saw no reason to withhold facts from citizens. During one debate, he said, "I don't know the smooth language lawyers use, but somebody's lyin'."

At a hearing that concerned the budget of a state facility, he asked a question to which the facility official replied, "Well, Senator, that's privileged information."

"I don't care nothing about privileged information," Ralph growled. "What is the truth?"

That was Ralph's question about every issue that confronted him. He wanted the truth. He wanted to know what the experts knew. Dr. Donald Stedman remembers Ralph calling him with questions about mental health legislation. He says:

I'M SURE HE HAD A WHOLE NETWORK of people he'd call from time to time and say, "What do you think about this?" He wanted to make sure he wasn't getting "hoodooed" as he called it.

His manner of speaking was all Moon Pies and Dr. Pepper. But underneath was a sharp, empathetic man with a quick mind and a heart of gold.

He was once dismayed about someone's lack of interest in creating more training for retarded children. I remember we were walking down the hall after having met with this individual and he said to me, "You can really find out a lot about a man when you start messing with his pocketbook."

Ralph described most lobbyists as "a bunch of hogs rootin' at the trough." And he was equally blunt in his comments about individuals. When a woman asked his opinion of North Carolina's Republican Senator Jesse Helms, he said that, "I told her if she wasn't for nothin' or nobody, he's the man."

He never tried to get out of responsibility for a comment he had made or a stand he had taken even if, later on, he might think better of it. He once said:

NEWSPAPERS HAVE NEVER quoted me incorrectly. I have said an awful lot of things that I wish I had never said, but I don't blame it on the newspapers. They were just doing their job.

There was only one person who could temper his comments. That was his wife. Every now and then he'd tell a story to newspaper columnist Jack Aulis that was something less than genteel. Like the one he told during the time in the 1970s when streaking had become a nationwide fad.

He said that he was against streaking, not because he was old and prudish, but because he was jealous. He even mentioned, with a grin, that he heard they had caught a girl streaking through the legislature. "They caught her," he said, "but they couldn't pin anything on her."

When stories like that would end up in the next day's *News and Observer*, Ralph would tell Jack that they had better not talk about such topics again "because Hazeleene doesn't like me to tell those things."

For all his love of talking, he was a man of few words and he admired that trait in others. He once commented about a long-winded colleague in the Senate, "I'm gonna remind him that the Lord gave him two ears but only one mouth."

On another occasion, when the folks on one side of an issue had let their emotions get out of hand, Ralph said, "A lot of times the ones who've got the most religion ain't the ones whoopin' and hollerin' on the street corner."

He didn't need many words to make his point. As his reputation grew, it was often enough for other legislators to know which side he was on. During a session in which he was working to get a big appropriations bill approved, he told the senators, "If you have any questions, I'll try to answer them but I won't guarantee it." The bill passed without further discussion.

He was driven by loyalty, to family and to people who had helped him. As long as their cause was just and honest, he was in their corner for the count. Dr. Bill Roberts remembers when he was a professor at N.C. State and was called to testify before a joint committee meeting. The issue concerned research being done at the college to remove the onion flavor from milk. Roberts told the committee that this research could save the state's dairy farmers about 50 cents per hundred pounds of milk. One legislator asked to be recognized and then said, "Mr. Chairman, I'd like to ask the learned professor a question. I'd like to ask him how he arrived at that figure."

Before Roberts could open his mouth to reply, Ralph got up and said, "I'd like to answer that question. I don't know nothing' about how he arrived at that figure. One thing I do know: if it hadn't been for the help he gave us, I wouldn't be in business today."

The other senator said, "Mr. Chairman, that's all I wanted to know." He was satisfied that if Ralph Scott knew this professor and believed in him, he must be all right.

Ralph always empathized with people in new situations and always wanted to ease difficult times for them. Senate colleague Marshall Rauch remembered one of those times in a letter to Ralph:

> . . . I WILL NEVER FORGET my first year in the Senate when I believe I got up on the floor and said something I probably should not have said. Voit Gilmore started to take me to task for saying it and I remember very well that you got up and minimized the entire situation, and in fact protected me. You have always been a strong defender of anyone in trouble or in need and I am so proud to have served in the General Assembly with you.

Tom White, a legend among the greats on the North Carolina Senate rolls, remembers Ralph from their college days. He says:

WE SAT ON THE BACK SEAT of the same English class. But I did not have the privilege of being thrown with him then except for that class.

Their friendship began to grow when White was elected to the State Senate in 1961. He eventually became chairman of the Finance Commiteee while Ralph was chairman of Appropriations. White remembers:

RALPH WAS A FRIEND you could count on. When he told you he'd do something, he did it. A good, sound, stable man.

And he was one of the wittiest people I've ever known. He was good at breaking up the tension of a heated debate. I remember once he got up in the Senate during a lull and asked to be recognized. Then, apropos of nothing, he said, "Mr. President, we got some people over at Haw River that have a son in Harvard University. At church the other Sunday, some of the neighbors were asking them about it and they said, 'We understand you got a son at Harvard University.' And the man said, 'Yeah, we do.' So the neighbor said, 'Well, what's he studyin' up there?' And the man said, 'Oh, he ain't studyin' nothin'. They's studyin' him.'"

Ralph could always sense an impasse and he could usually get around it with a story like that. He knew how to avoid an argument that was headed for more heat than light.

Ralph and Tom White became a formidable team in the Senate. After they had worked closely together during a particularly difficult session, Ralph said that if White didn't end up with ulcers, it was only because "his guts is too tough to make chitlins."

Monk Harrington was another longtime Senate colleague. He first met Ralph in 1948 when he was a proud member of the branch head boys who successfully worked for Kerr's election. Harrington says:

> I HAD A FRIEND WHO was helping me to work for Kerr Scott in our little town of Lewiston. When we won the town of Lewiston for Kerr Scott against the big wheels, we were just really thrilled to death. And we came up to a big barbecue that Kerr Scott gave. We rode all the way up to Alamance County for it.

But, like White, Harrington did not come to know Ralph well until his own election to the State Senate in 1962. That was when, says Harrington, he and Ralph became close friends:

> RALPH HELPED ME every time I needed advice. We had a friendship that seemed to develop automatically that went back to his brother. That friendship kept getting larger during all our years in the Senate. We didn't vote alike on everything — in those days, we didn't keep up with how you voted on everything the way we do nowadays. But you

could always depend on Ralph coming through with the common sense viewpoint and looking out for the average people and poor people. Ralph always said what he was thinking whether it was popular or not. When he got up and talked on the Senate floor, we all paid close attention. He carried a lot of weight with the senators. He was a big power to reckon with.

Basically, Ralph was pretty easy to get along with. He didn't try to pick fights with people. He got along with people. That was part of the basis of his power, that he got along with people. He had his right and wrong, legislation that he didn't believe in and he let you know he didn't believe in it too. But he would fight for the ones he believed in. That kept him at the top of popularity and respect of all the senators. Ralph was respected as much as any senator I can remember.

That says a lot, considering how long he stayed in the Senate. And I really can't think of where he has ever been so far off base that people have been critical of him. He didn't win all his cases, but he got his share.

Ralph would not compromise too easy. He was a man of high principles. He would not bend to the establishment, you might say. He was a man of high principles and he would hold up for those principles too. He could always defend his position.

Ralph made his defense with reason and humor rather than fire and fury, which is probably why he usually won the argument. "Don't never get so mad it loses you what you want," he'd say.

Opponents could not escape his wit. They often turned up at Monk Harrington's annual deer hunt, an important event for every Democrat who has or hopes to have power and influence in the state. Ralph went to the hunt each year, not for the sport since he was never known to hunt an animal, but because he loved the company and the talk and the politicking. Just before this event one year, Geneva Warren, who was a family friend, asked him if he was going down there to hunt. "Naw," he replied. "I ain't got nothin' against them deer. I'm an eatin' delegate!"

Russell Clay worked with Ralph during most of his Senate career. He says:

RALPH IS KNOWN FOR his blunt talk and penetrating wit. His barbs smart but they don't do any damage because he tosses them without rancor. That's the way he is. He is one of the few totally good people I have known.

Once a fellow senator was espousing a piece of self-serving legislation. Ralph got up and, fiddling with his tie as he so often did, he said, "I don't mind the senator going to the public trough, but he ought not to get in it lengthwise and wallow."

One time he received a letter from a constituent. It was a scurrilous letter raising hell about Kerr and Bob and Ralph. Ralph sent the letter right back with a note that said, "Look what some fool has signed your name to."

Beneath all the levity is a Ralph Scott of serious purpose. He spearheaded progressive legislation for 30 years, championing the cause of education and mental health. He got a Homestead Exemption law for old folks put on the books. He was an ecologist before ecology was cool. He was trying to clean up the Haw River long before cleaning up rivers became the popular thing to do.

And he is one of the gentlest people who ever walked the earth.

He held his adversaries in check by the soundness of his argument and the keenness of his wit. Probably his greatest strength is his ability to present his facts and arguments in language easily understood by his hearers. The most unlettered folks in his audience went away with some fact he had embedded in his words.

His favorite poem is "The Bridge Builder" about the old man building a bridge for the young one. He would quote from it often in his speeches.

You know, there's the whole world and then there's Ralph Scott.

His personality and character turned political foes into personal supporters. Republican colleagues like Senator Reid Poovey, who calls Ralph "one of my best friends," valued his forthright manner and came to depend on his blunt honesty.

Another colleague, Lindsay Warren, Jr., remembers those qualities:

I HAD THE PLEASURE of serving with Ralph Scott in the State Senate for four terms in the 1960s. I had not known Senator Scott personally before that date but knew him by reputation. My deceased father served with him in the 1959 and 1961 Senates. I knew from him what a unique personality Ralph Scott is. Apart from his well-known humor, the thing I remember most about Senator Scott is his loyalty to his friends and the integrity of his word. In a legislative body, you find out a lot about human nature. As in most situations in life, you find people you can count on and others that you cannot. Ralph was always one that you could count on. If he gave you his word, you could feel confident that he would stand by it no matter how difficult it might be for him at the time of decision. Sometimes when he got into a controversial piece of legislation, he would tell me, "Let me know what you want me to do." I always considered that a compliment coming from Ralph Scott....

Ralph was not only loyal to his friends, but he was loyal to his convictions and beliefs. He was not afraid to take an unpopular stand if he believed in it. Because of this, he frequently received the condemnation and cynicism of his enemies and others who failed to understand. I always admired this trait in him even though I didn't always agree with his position.

Ralph never minced words. In 1964 he supported Richardson Preyer in the Democratic gubernatorial primary against Dan Moore. He was outspoken in his criticism of Moore who, according to Ralph, had too many fat cats in his camp. "And when the fat cats are meetin' you can bet they ain't worried about your problems," he'd tell campaign crowds.

Ralph believed that a representative for the people should be one of the people. He decried the change from biennial to annual sessions of the legislature. "We could end up with professionals," he said. "Too many lawyers down there representing clients."

He believed in listening to constituents and talking with them, even if he disagreed. That earned him the respect of those whom he openly opposed. For instance, he worked fiercely for the rights of black citizens. Still, when a constituent from the local John Birch Society called him with a list of grievances, he told her to get her group together and he'd come talk to them.

He believed that the solution to problems lay in talk and reason and the democratic process, not in demonstrations and civil disobedience. "Defiance of law and order is self-defeating," he once said. At a gathering in 1982 in Alamance County to present an award to Ralph, Dr. S.B. Thomas talked about the relationship that the black community cherished with Ralph. Dr. Thomas said in his speech:

> I WANT TO [talk about] the time when things weren't so pleasant in Alamance County . . . the fifties and the sixties when the climate was rather hostile and the relationship between the races was strained. And there were very few white people we

felt we could trust. . . . During all this time, we were rapping with the Senator. He trusted us and we trusted him. It was through him and his influence and his understanding of our problems that we accomplished things without publicity. Senator Scott proved to be a friend. He stuck his neck way out — and what was good about it, he didn't have to do it. We knew the Senator had repercussions because of his association with us.

Repercussions never daunted Ralph. Regardless of the situation, he never hesitated to stick his neck out for someone or something he believed in.

Anne Queen says that Ralph "was absolutely fearless." Indeed he was, for he viewed fear as destructive and dangerous. He once wrote a colleague about some legislation which he supported. "Of course, they are trying to kill it with fear," he wrote, "which is, as you know, the easiest way to kill anything."

Jack Aulis says of Ralph:

HE WAS NOT SHY about telling you what he would do or wouldn't do and when he said he would do something, he did it.

People felt he had enormous personal integrity and political integrity. He had great compassion for people and for causes that affected people. And when he felt something strongly, he said, "I'm for that" or "I'm against that" and he stuck to his guns.

One of Ralph's earliest opportunities to stick out his neck and stick to his guns came in 1953 when he introduced the Milk Commission bill in the General Assembly. The bill, which set up a commission to regulate the price farmers got for their milk, became a dartboard for many of the state's newspapers. The *Winston-Salem Journal* let one missile fly in an editorial that called the bill anti-competitive. Ralph wrote the editor a letter in which he observed that the *Journal* was owned by a company that also owned the town's other newspaper as well as a local television station and radio station. So, Ralph wrote, that company had solved the problem of competition, and dairies wanted to do the same. The Milk Commission legislation was one of the first examples of Ralph's persuasiveness and determination to hold out for what he believed was right. After much debate, the bill was enacted.

In 1963 Ralph took on another cause that was to become the talk of the state. That year, the General Assembly passed a bill known as the Speaker Ban Law, which prohibited speakers on college and university campuses if they were Communist party members or known subversives or had ever taken the Fifth Amendment on questions regarding possible Communist or subversive activities. The fires of controversy over that law raged across the state for two years.

Ralph was one of the most vocal opponents of the speaker ban. He believed the matter should be left to the schools themselves. He said that under the ban:

FIDEL CASTRO COULD SPEAK, because he claims he isn't a Communist. Robert E. Lee couldn't speak because he advocated the overthrow of the U.S. Constitution by force. This is the way of the coward. . . . To support this bill is to say that you don't believe in the power of human reason. . . . This kind of legislation is always the last ditch stand of fearful people who are afraid to argue with their enemies.

The Speaker Ban Law threatened to cost the state's schools their accreditation. Ralph opposed the ban for that reason too and said so. He wrote to the *Burlington Times-News*:

CAN ANY REASONABLE PERSON, after weighing the chaos and the frustration and injury to students that would result from the loss of accreditation, object to that kind of amendment [to give each school responsibility for its own speakers]? I could not object to it and still sleep at night, knowing that I had a hand in helping to tear down schools for which dedicated people have literally given their lives. . . . I am going to keep on fighting for the welfare of the University, for the future of our children, and for the good name of North Carolina. To do less would be to disgrace my family, the citizens of Alamance County, and the unborn generations who will reap the harvest of what we sow here.

For two years, Ralph never missed an opportunity to speak out on the speaker ban. In 1965 the law was amended as he proposed.

Thoughout his life, he never missed an opportunity to support better education. Like his father before him, he believed it was critical. When he finally retired from public life, he wrote to a friend:

> I DOUBT IF I WILL EVER run again, but I will miss working for education in all its phases. That's one thing we can do for our young people that no one can take away from them. All we can do for them is put the opportunity before them, and I am glad I have been able to help.

The Speaker Ban Law was one of many issues that put Ralph and Governor Moore on opposite sides. Some people said that Moore had a "quiet administration," but Ralph was characteristically more blunt. He later said of the governor:

> HE WAS THE RIGHT MAN at the right time. People wanted to stop and get their breath. They were ready for a governor who wouldn't do nothin'.

Once during that administration, supporters of Moore attacked Ralph for his criticism. In reply, Ralph wrote:

> CERTAINLY, I HAVE CRITICIZED Governor Dan Moore when I thought he was wrong. I will keep on doing that. The Governor, as the No. 1 citizen of the state, has an obligation to take a stand on the No. 1 issues, and they won't go away if he

turns his back on them. When leadership is entrusted to a man, he either accepts it or rejects it. He can no more remain neutral or stand still than can a cowboy who sees a stampede coming his way. Serious affairs of state, when serious decisions are pending, do not get on a treadmill and wait for a Governor to decide whether he will or he won't do something. . . . It is interesting to me to hear all the howling about my criticism of the Governor, because most of it is coming from the same people who regularly took the hide off my brother, Kerr, when he was Governor. What they said about Kerr makes what I have said about Moore sound like a compliment.

As he championed the cause of black citizens and free speech, he also championed women's rights. He said that he didn't see a thing wrong with the ERA and he vigorously supported it. He said:

SOMETIMES WHEN I HEAR the phrase "women's liberation," I think it would be more accurate to say that it is we men who should be liberated from our ancient prejudices, based upon sex discrimination. I doubt if there's a sign on the pearly gates reading "Men Only."

Ralph not only championed causes but he was equally vocal in his support of individuals regardless of whether they were the most popular candidates. One such person for

whom he spoke out was John Stockard, a young Alamance
County native who ran for sheriff in 1962. Stockard says of
Ralph:

> HE WAS ONE OF THE FEW men who thought I had
> a chance and he went to bat for me all out with his
> influence as well as financially. I couldn't have
> made it without him.

Stockard won that election, and he has been continuously
re-elected Alamance County sheriff ever since. His memories
of Ralph go back to his childhood when the two families
were friends. He recalls:

> HE SEEMED TO TAKE YOU under his wing if he
> liked you. And he helped many a young kid in this
> county, a lot of them that people didn't know
> about. Helping them get jobs or get into school or
> helping them in any way he could. And he's the
> type of individual that wanted to be anonymous.
> He wasn't looking for praise. He's not that kind of
> man.
>
> He was one of the few men that if he told you
> something, you could count on it. If he said, "I'm
> going to do this," he would. I would rather have
> his word than a contract.
>
> He was the type of individual that I could sit
> down and disagree with and still admire the man.
> He didn't want you to be a yes-man. If you had
> opposition to what he was wanting to do, express
> your opinions. That didn't necessarily mean you
> were going to change his mind.

He was very sympathetic to blacks and they respected him. But there again, he was the type that if he told you he was going to do something, you could bet he was going to do it if possible. He would make an honest effort. And if he couldn't do it, he would explain to you why he couldn't.

I've heard this all my life, that he was always one to help people. They would line up outside his office in Burlington on Saturdays. They would line up to come to see him with their problems and he would always have time to listen to them. I never heard of his refusing to listen to anyone.

We would try to get him to run for governor but he would say, "No, I can do more good where I am." And I'll tell you the truth, in his prime, he had more power and more influence than the governor had, especially when he was chairman of Appropriations. If you wanted something done in Raleigh, Mr. Ralph would get it done. If I wanted to see the governor, I'd go to Mr. Ralph and he'd get me in to see the governor, even after he left the Senate.

And he'd call me ever so often and say, "John, come down here and eat breakfast with me." And I'd go down there and there'd be somebody like Jim Hunt or somebody from the Senate, and Miss Hazeleene would have a breakfast cooked.

He was not one to get out and beat the bushes just before an election. I think he did his politicking every day. Not like a politician who takes two or three months and just floods the county. He didn't do that. He did his every day and by doing little things for people. People remember that.

If you had a political gathering, you could be sure he was going to be there. And we had many, many rallies at his farm. We cooked many a hotdog out there, often in October before the election.

He used to open his farm up every time dove season would open. He'd have dove hunts — although he never went hunting himself — and then they'd usually have a big cookout and Miss Hazeleene would feed us there at their house. It might be 50 or 75 or 100 people and they'd feed us.

He wasn't like a lot of politicians who tell you something to get rid of you or maybe to get something back in return. He's not that type. I think his power came from respect. People respected him and knew that if he told you something, you could count on it.

You could count on Ralph to never compromise his views or his position. Still, he understood the value of political partnerships, of working with an opponent to achieve your goals. In 1972 Jim Holshouser was elected North Carolina's first Republican governor in this century. Afterwards, Ralph lamented that the Democrats lost because their candidate refused to mend fences with another wing of the Democratic party. Said Ralph:

HE DIDN'T WANT TO BE obligated to [them] so he didn't make any effort to get their support. He beat himself. Nobody else beat him.

As for working with Holshouser while he was governor, Ralph said, "After he was elected . . . I figured it was to Alamance County's advantage for me to work with him."

Ralph took the well-being of his constituents very seriously and he was intense in his determination to help citizens throughout the state. But he never took himself seriously, even when his power and influence became legendary. After serving nearly two decades in the Senate, someone asked him why he didn't file earlier one year for re-election. Ralph said that he was waiting for somebody to ask him to run and nobody did, so he decided he'd better go ahead and file.

He did, and he won. In fact, Ralph, the progressive populist, kept on winning elections even though Alamance County was notably conservative. His margin of victory was sometimes small, but it was still a victory. In 1970 he won the election by only 13 votes. "Hell, it was 12 more votes than I needed," he said and began calling himself "Landslide Scott."

The election of 1972 demonstrated Ralph's unique relationship with his constituents. North Carolina voters that year elected a Republican governor (Jim Holshouser), put a Republican in Kerr's old U.S. Senate seat (Jesse Helms), and all but two counties in the state (Orange and Northampton) voted for a Republican president (Richard Nixon). Yet Ralph was elected once again to the State Senate.

Ralph undoubtedly could have looked for other, higher political offices but, after returning to the legislature in 1961, he never did.

Jack Aulis explains it this way:

THE THING THAT INTRIGUES ME most about Ralph, other than the fact that he is absolutely one of the nicest people I've ever met, is that he has always had these other family members who were in higher positions than he was, and it never seemed to make any difference to him. I have the feeling that Ralph knew what he was doing and what he wanted to be. I don't think he ever wanted to be anything other than what he was. I don't think he was envious of them or jealous of them. I think he saw what he was doing as equally important or more important. And he always worked with them. But he was never a shadow. He was always his own person.

In 1964 friends tried to get him to become Commissioner of Agriculture. L.Y. (Stag) Ballentine, who had become the commissioner in 1948 when Kerr left the job to be governor, died in office that year. But when he was asked to consider the position, Ralph said, "No, Jim Graham is the man for that job." And he threw his considerable influence behind Graham's appointment. In return, he asked Graham for only one thing. "Just promise me you'll always do what you think is right," Ralph said, "and best for the people."

That was always Ralph's foremost concern: what was best for the people; what would help them to get an education, get a job, get health care services, get the ear of those who controlled their future. During the 1964 campaign, a group of supporters who called themselves "Parents for Scott" ran a newspaper advertisement that said in part:

SELDOM HAS ANYONE SOUGHT an appointment with Senator Scott on matters involving Alamance County and state government but that he has found the time to give it. He takes people to Raleigh to see that they are placed in contact with the right authorities to follow through with their interests, concerns, and problems. If he doesn't make the trip with them, he sees that they are granted appointments with those who are directly associated with the issues in question. This is a valuable service to our area, and it is a valuable asset when one of such position gives his time so freely to the people in helping them meet their needs. . . . We need his keen understanding of the dignity of the individual."

Dignity of the individual. Ralph saw that dignity in every child and adult, black or white, man or woman. Dignity that he believed should be fought for and maintained and strengthened. So he dedicated his life to that fight.

IV

PEOPLE OF HAWFIELDS REMEMBER

D.J. Walker, Jr., a prominent Burlington attorney grew up in that town and his memories of Ralph begin early:

I REMEMBER RALPH WHEN he first got out of college and was working at the dairy. He was doing the delivery of milk. He used to bring it to our house when it was in glass bottles. He always tried to put it in the shade so the sun wouldn't get to it.

We got milk every day. I was a little boy then, living in Burlington. Daddy was the clerk of the court at that time.

When I came home from World War II, I went to law school. Then I decided to run for clerk of the court. I wrote about 25 or 30 letters to people I knew because I didn't have any money. Among those people was Ralph Scott. I got $100 — my uncle gave me $50 and so did Ralph. That money helped me to put some ads in the paper. Then I bought a few cards on my own to hand out and I won the election. Stayed in that job for five years.

That first year I got elected was 1948, the same year that Kerr was elected governor. That was a doubtful year for the Democrats because the Republicans had been beating us all over, even in Alamance County in 1946, and that was unheard of back then. They got two Alamance County commissioners and the sheriff, so we were out to beat them in 1948. Truman was running against Dewey that year and everybody thought Dewey was going to win. It was even announced that he had won on election night and then we woke up the next morning to find Truman had won instead.

We weren't worried about Kerr winning that year and he did. We won all the county offices back too, by the usual 2 to 1 margin.

After I became clerk of the court, one of the county commissioners resigned. Now the clerk appoints the successor, so I appointed Ralph and he agreed to accept. He had already been county commissioner once and he agreed to take this appointment for a four-year term. But then, with Kerr being governor, Ralph decided that he needed to run for the General Assembly at the next election, which was 1950.

After he was elected to the Senate, I went down there one time to visit and he introduced me on the floor by remembering that he was holding the seat that my daddy had held 20 years before.

Ralph had a great interest in mental health and in handicapped people. He and John Umstead together built up our state mental health system with Ralph working particularly for the mentally retarded.

I had a brother with Downs syndrome and Ralph and his family were always real helpful about him. They helped my mother a lot too. For instance, my sister went to school with Ralph's daughter Miriam at UNC-Greensboro. Ralph and his family were always going to Greensboro to see Miriam and they were always taking Mama with them to see my sister.

We were finally able to get my brother into Murdoch Center [a state facility for the mentally retarded] and Ralph was instrumental in that. He also got some legislation adopted that says, in effect, that the state will take care of its mentally handicapped people and the parents don't have to bear the burden. The cost to parents had always been tremendous, so that was a great thing he did. And he did so much more. The state's mental facilities are now wonderful. They teach people who have no skills and very little mental ability to do things and take care of themselves. All of that is largely due to Ralph.

I know my family was grateful to him, and we are typical of so many people in North Carolina. I continually meet somebody who will bring up the fact that they have a mentally handicapped person in the family who has benefitted from something

Ralph did. They ought to name one of the buildings for the mentally retarded after him because he has done so much without getting the credit for it.

He didn't have any personal interest in these services. He just knew we needed them and he was stubborn about it and, by golly, he got them. Ralph comes from that strong Democratic, Presbyterian background. And all of the Scotts are as stubborn as hell — you couldn't back them off from anything they wanted to do!

Now Ralph is a real nice guy, but he's going to get what he sets out for. And in the legislature, everybody knew not to mess with him because he knew the ropes and knew how to work them.

Ralph has gotten a lot of criticism and the Scott family has gotten a lot of criticism for all of them holding public office. But you know, a generation or two before it was the Shelby crowd in Raleigh and O. Max Gardner had his whole family down there and he was brother-in-law to Clyde Hoey who was governor four years later. People who want to fight you just pick on those things and they are not valid at all because the Scotts have meant a lot to North Carolina. They have just done wonders for this state.

Ralph always believed in letting people know what you stand for instead of promising them things. I once heard him criticize somebody who was running for the State House of Representatives. The candidate promised somebody something and Ralph said, "Now you've lost all the votes of the people who were against that thing. And on top of that, if you do get elected and go down there, the bill for that thing may never come up. And if it does come up, it may not get out of committee. And if it does get out of committee, you won't be called on to vote for it until it comes up on the floor. And it may be defeated. And here you've gone and promised it."

Ralph is also a great family man. He was crazy about his wife and loves his children. You know, his daughter married a Republican, but I understand she doesn't vote with him!

In 1981, the Senior Opportunities and Services of Alamance County wanted to honor Ralph, so they asked me to write an inscription for the plaque to be presented to him. So I wrote that it was for being "a champion of those who have no champion — the handicapped, the needy and the disadvantaged." Later Miriam took me out to the cemetery. Ralph had wanted his tombstone put up and they had put my words on it. I felt greatly honored.

Nowadays, a champion is somebody who wins top honors. But a champion in the olden tournament days was a person who fought for some cause and that was what I meant about Ralph.

And he has stayed the same from the time I first knew him as a young man.

Like Walker, Betsy Warren Harrison first remembers Ralph when she was still a child:

Ralph H. Scott

I FIRST REMEMBER SEEING Ralph Scott at my father's funeral at the graveside. I later asked someone who that man was who was crying so hard. From that point on, he was just always [part of] our lives. I suppose he was concerned about my mom being a widow with four children to raise and he stepped in to help the family of a friend. It would be some time before I realized that I got my first lesson in loyalty that day.

If there is one word that summarizes Ralph Scott and the life he lived or a motto to which he held, it would be loyalty. He believed in loyalty, whether to an old friend, the Democratic party, a certain state cause, or Alamance County. And he lived it every day of his life. . . .

He was never the same after [Hazeleene's] death. . . . Truly they were sweethearts to the end. She was a sweet, genteel, soft-spoken Southern lady whom he delighted in shocking with his outspoken ways. I can just hear her saying, "Oh, Ralph" right now and smiling like a shy school girl at something outlandish he said. I think most of the sentences he used started with "I told Hazeleene . . . ." He has been lost without her. . . .

We [used to eat] at the Western Steak House in Burlington. For a couple of years in a row, he pointed out their "KC Special Steak". . . . I was puzzled over why he was crazy about such a little piece of steak. Then when all of us were served it, I realized what was happening. His "KC Special Steak" was about four or five times the size of ours. The owners were looking out for him because he was "Mr. Ralph" and because he had helped them along the way. . . .

He loved to go to the Farmers Market with Jim Graham and Melvin Hearn and others to eat streak-of-lean. He loved being a member of the "Chitlin Club" where members were held in contempt if they were seen in public enjoying any sort of culture whatsoever.

He always tipped heaviest at the small restaurants like Your House in Raleigh. I asked him one day why he left such a big tip at those places and he said, "They don't do this [for a living] 'cause they like to." Always the champion of the underdog. Always.

[I remember when] my mother was fuming over what to do about several candidates for the same office who were asking for her support. "Just tell all of them you'll do all you can for them," he said.

He had the most complaints from people who had family members in prison. He was very sympathetic, and unless the crime was violent, didn't hold too much with keeping someone in prison and away from their families for a long time. . . .

The clinic at Prospect Hill where my mother lives has a copper plaque inscribed to Senator Scott, citing his help when he was chairman of Appropriations in getting funds for the site. I know that he has touched thousands of lives with a kind of generosity that is so totally unselfish. . . .

He has taught me about loyalty and politics the way it should be done and humor and not to take myself too seriously. He has shown me what is really important in this world.

Ralph's unselfishness was evident in many aspects of the lives of Alamance County citizens. For years, he made sure that every patient in the Burlington hospital got a copy of the local newspaper every day. He sent letters of congratulations to people who were honored for some educational achievement or community deed. He would cut out the newspaper clipping about the honor and send it to the person or, in the case of youngsters, to their parents. He liked to help young people get into college in any way he could. He once received a letter from the mother of a student he had helped which said:

WE WOULD LIKE TO EXPRESS our gratitude for the help you gave our son. . . . You used your influence in getting him admitted to Appalachian State University after he had been turned down for acceptance.

[He] was graduated last May with a degree in Management [and] was recruited and hired by a textile plant upon graduation. . . . [He] has done quite well with the company, having been promoted to supervisor after only 6 months on the job.

Again, we just want you to know how much we appreciate what you did for our son and that he didn't let you down or us and that he will be more equipped now to make a contribution to society. One person *can* make a difference in another's life!!! [Our son] wouldn't be in the position he is today if it had not been for you.

Ralph's generosity carried no thought of return. In fact, he refused it. He sent back one such gift with the following letter:

THANK YOU FOR YOUR RECENT letter with reference to your application for employment as a State highway patrol trooper.

I appreciate very much your thoughtfulness in sending a gift for my effort. However, I am returning it, and hope you will understand. I am always glad to be of help to my constituents in any way I can, and never want remuneration for it. The greatest pleasure I get out of life is helping others.

Otis Lackey's memories of Ralph go back to 1941 when Lackey was a college student and first met the man with whom he would work throughout his business career:

THE FIRST TIME I MET Senator Scott was at N.C. State. I was a student. It was the spring of 1941. I was completing my work at college and I had been working there in the dairy department. The head of the department was always looking out for Ralph. That was Professor William Clevenger, head of Dairy Manufacturing, now called the Food Science Department.

Professor Clevenger said to me that Ralph Scott from Melville Dairy in Burlington was coming down to the campus looking for somebody because he had decided the time had come to employ a field man. I'm not sure I even knew exactly what he had reference to but what it was, of course, was somebody representing the dairy who would contact prospective dairy farmers who were called milk producers.

I never will forget that Professor Clevenger said Ralph had been bidding for some time on military contracts at Fort Bragg. The buildup had already started [for the war]. Professor Clevenger said that Ralph wanted to keep his name on the list of bids but he hardly had enough milk to supply his customers in Alamance County. And then all of a sudden, he got a military contract and he didn't have any milk to fill it.

Professor Clevenger was a very close advisor to Ralph. In fact, I guess Ralph would give the professor credit for everything he ever accomplished in his dairy business, that was how fond Ralph was of him. And he had been Ralph's teacher at N.C. State. Ralph thought so much of him that he named one of his sons after him.

Anyway, Professor Clevenger said that he and Ralph had decided that the time had come for him to get a field man to work with the farmers and try to get a better and larger raw milk supply for Melville Dairy. They called it "building up the Burlington milkshed."

I said that I would certainly be glad to meet Ralph and talk about it. So in March or April of 1941, Professor Clevenger got Ralph and me together there at the college. I remember Ralph said that very little grade A milk was being produced in Alamance County. Tobacco was the principle agricultural interest in the county along with cotton. Of course, there were the Scott family dairy operations. Kerr had a big dairy herd and another brother Henry did too and so did Ralph.

So Ralph and I talked about the job. It was the only job interview I ever had. We must have reached some kind of agreement because I came to Burlington. The first day I reported for work I probably didn't talk to Ralph more than ten minutes before he headed me out to Lexington where Coble Dairy was doing quite a bit of expanding at the time. I spent the rest of that first day touring some farms around there. I didn't get back to Burlington until night. And it suddenly occurred to me that I hadn't made arrangements whatsoever about where I was going to sleep that night. Ralph and I hadn't even gotten around to talking about that. He was so lowkey. There was no high pressure, no promises. Everything was very lowkey.

So while I was eating supper at Cole's Restaurant that night, I looked through the classified ads and saw there was a room to rent out on West Davis

Street and I ended up going out there and staying there until I went into the service.

I spent my time with the dairy calling on farmers in Alamance County, learning the names of people who might be prospective producers and then going to talk with them. I got very little instructions from Ralph. What little he said was quite clear, and the longer I knew him the better I understood that he meant what he said and you never had to wonder about it.

I've heard that called bluntness or the opposite of diplomacy. Whatever you want to call it, he was very frank and straightforward about everything. He would grunt a few times and actually say very little about how he wanted something done. He usually left it pretty much up to me. He just said that "We've got to have some more milk producers and you're gonna have to get out here and talk some of these tobacco farmers into milking a few cows."

It was hard to do. Most of them had a family cow. But there sure weren't many of them interested in being confined to milk producing. I always thought tobacco farming was pretty confining, but I remember some of them would say to me, "You're standing here talking about something that's gonna keep me home seven days a week."

There were some of them who were selling cream. You'd drive down an old rural road in those days — they weren't paved because that was before Kerr Scott paved our roads — and there would be an old ten-gallon milkcan, or sometimes a couple of fives — sitting out at the mailbox, sitting there in July sun or February snow.

Ralph told me not to oversell what we were trying to do. We had to instill in them the desire to produce a good quality product. During the next ten or twelve months, we accomplished what we set out to do and we got enough producers to fill the Fort Bragg contract.

Then I went in the Navy and when I came back, I never really had any other thought than to come back to Ralph. He said he would like for me to get into the sales aspect then. He later said he wanted to change my title to Assistant Manager so I could get a little bit more involved in all aspects of the business. By then, he was away a great deal of time, in the legislature. He got involved in a lot of committee work there, so he continued to go to Raleigh pretty much the year around.

In the morning, he'd always stop at the post office for the mail and then go on down to the dairy. That would be one of the times I'd be sitting there in his office, and he'd open his mail and there'd be a note from somebody and he'd hand it to me to read and to smile or chuckle about with him.

Lackey ended up keeping many of those little notes and they became part of a touching collection of Melville Dairy memorabilia, illustrating the close relationship Ralph built up with his customers and constituents.

Lackey also received letters from people who became part of the life of Melville Dairy. One in particular he remembers because it came from a young woman that Ralph's nephew Bob had talked to him about. Bob said that she was pretty special and would really be an asset to the dairy in a summer job when she got out of college. Lackey hired her and, at the end of the summer, received this handwritten note from her:

Mr. Lackey,

I want to thank you for "taking me in" last June right after I finished school. It has been very interesting, enjoyable, and educational working here. I'm sure the experience is going to be helpful in teaching. And, incidentally, I'll be sure to sing the praises of Melville milk wherever I am.

Thank you again for allowing me the privilege of working with such fine people.

Jessie Rae

Lackey saved the note, not realizing it was from Bob's future wife and a future First Lady of North Carolina.

Like Lackey, Melvin Hearn had just graduated from N.C. State and was waiting for the draft when he first met Ralph. The year was 1942. Hearn's former professor, William Clevenger, called him one day and asked if he would like to go up to Burlington to help Mr. Scott with his field work. Clevenger said that Otis Lackey was going into the Navy and someone was needed to take his place because Melville Dairy was trying to build a milkshed.

Hearn said that he was expecting the Army to call him any time but that he would be glad to help until then. So in April 1942 he went with Professor Clevenger from Raleigh to Burlington, met with Ralph, and talked with Otis Lackey about the job. Afterwards, Ralph followed his usual custom with visitors — he took them to the local Western Cafe for a broiled steak lunch.

After lunch, Hearn remembers that they were standing beside the car, ready to leave when Ralph said, "We haven't talked about a salary."

Professor Clevenger said, "Well, Ralph, he won't be able to buy a car in this short period of time. I suggest you buy him a car and pay him $100 a month."

Ralph said that was fine and the contract was sealed with his word. In August, the Army drafted Hearn and he left without any discussion about Ralph taking him back when the war was over. But when Lackey and Hearn received their military discharges, they both came back to this man who had become a friend and both found their old jobs waiting for them.

Professor Clevenger next advised Ralph on some new steps to take to expand his business. Accordingly, Ralph put Lackey in charge of sales and gave all the field work to Hearn.

In the midst of this expansion, Kerr began considering a race for governor. Lexie Ray remembered how Ralph encouraged his brother to run:

AT A MEETING OF a small group at Melville Dairy in Burlington, a report was made on a survey that had been conducted across the state testing Kerr's

chances of winning. . . . The report was: you can't
make it. Ralph asked Kerr what he planned to do
if he didn't run. He said he [would come] back to
his farm and continue in the dairy business. Ralph
said, "This won't delay it but six months. Let's go!"

The branch head boys came to life. There are
dozens of interesting stories . . . like the "Coble
breakfast" we had at the Alamance Hotel with
Kerr, Ralph, George White from Raleigh, George
Coble, and Ray Coltrane, trying to get George
Coble's support before Kerr announced for
governor. After a nice breakfast and some frank
discussion, George and his brother-in-law left the
room for a conference in the hallway. In a few
minutes they returned and George — in his usual
blustery fashion — announced that he was going
to support Kerr for governor and he was putting
in a sizeable contribution and meant to win. Then
he added, "Kerr, I want you to do one thing for
me. Don't tell anyone for three weeks that I am
supporting you because I've called you a S.O.B. to
everybody from the Virginia line to South Carolina
and I need some time to tell them it ain't so."

Kerr's election and Ralph's subsequent political career
did not halt the expansion of Melville Dairy. Hearn remembers those days as a time of unique satisfaction. Ralph's
leadership style was clearly the result of his youthful days,
working side by side with the laborers on his father's farm.
His employees became an extension of his family. His
customers became friends whom he cared about and they

returned the feeling, often writing him little notes with their monthly payments to thank him for some special service or to share with him a favorite Bible verse.

Ralph was always looking for ways to modernize and improve his business. A handwritten note from a customer in 1963 says:

> I AM DELIGHTED that orders can be given over a recording telephone. Progress I call it!

But he favored progress only if it meant better service to the people. Milk deliveries, which had originally been made seven days a week, were cut back to three days a week during World War II because of shortages and transportation problems. That schedule continued at Melville Dairy until 1967 when Ralph realized that another change needed to be made. It had become increasingly difficult to find competent route salesmen willing to deliver milk six days a week (handling two routes at three days a week each). Ralph didn't like the idea of reducing service to the people he served. So he wrote a long letter to each customer, explaining the situation in detail and he closed by saying:

> NEEDLESS TO SAY, we will do anything possible to prevent this arrangement from working a hardship on you. . . . We could ask no greater favor of you than to have you consider this change and the reasons for it and then let [us] know if it is . . . agreeable to you.

In 1968 Ralph sold Melville Dairy to Guilford Dairy of Greensboro, which had been co-founded by his brother Kerr. By that time, Ralph had built his business into more than a milk processing and delivery operation. It was an Alamance County institution.

The people of Hawfields and neighboring areas remember the Melville Dairy Pony Hitch, a sprightly team of six Shetland ponies who pulled a small wagon around Ralph's farm on special occasions. Customers delighted in bringing their children out for a ride on one of the ponies. In June 1958 the local newspaper carried headlines that said "Crowd of Over 2500 Views Melville Ponies on Scott Farm Saturday" and the article described how "Melville Dairy gave away ice cream and punch to the huge throng turning out for the occasion, exceeding all expectations."

The people of Hawfields remember the Melville Dairy bar on the ground floor of the Burlington plant. It became a popular lunch spot where the favorite dessert was pound cake topped with peaches, ice cream, and chocolate syrup. Thick, freshly made ice cream sandwiches sold for a dime and were well worth a trip downtown on a hot summer afternoon.

Despite his growing business and his long hours spent on legislative matters, Ralph always had time for people, for individuals. Melvin Hearn remembers many instances of his compassion and generosity to his neighbors. One example involved a man in the community who died in the early 1940s while his two daughters were in high school. The two girls managed to finish school and go on to graduate from what was then Woman's College in Greensboro. Years later, it became known that Ralph and his brother Jim had paid their way through school.

Another example concerned a local farmer who sold milk to Melville Dairy. Few people in those days, especially farmers, had hospital insurance. So when this man developed a serious case of appendicitis and went to the hospital for an operation, his family didn't know how they could ever pay the bill. They need not have worried. On the day of his discharge, when the farmer went to the hospital office to talk about what he owed, he was told that he didn't owe a penny. Someone had already taken care of his bill. It was much later that the farmer learned that his anonymous benefactor was Ralph Scott.

His neighbors remember other famous Ralph Scott trademarks such as feeding the squirrels on his farm and hosting cookouts for hundreds of people from the community. They remember his humor that was as much a part of his private life as his public one. It was a quiet, unaffected humor born of his plain-spoken upbringing. One day when his son Henderson was a youngster, working on the farm, he fell out of the silo and was consequently late for supper. When he finally got home, Ralph asked why he hadn't gotten there on time.

"Because I fell out of the silo," young Henderson explained.

Ralph replied that this was no excuse. "It don't take that long to fall out of a silo," he said.

Jim Graham says;

RALPH SCOTT IS NOT a "farmer" in the true sense of the word. He doesn't make his living that way, although he does think like a farmer. . . .

One day a neighbor of his said, "Ralph, I've got this cow that walks with a limp sometimes and at other times walks O.K. What do you think I should do?"

Ralph thought for a minute and said, "The next time she walks O.K., sell her."

Another time Ralph was putting up some kind of building on his place. Somebody asked him what he was building and Ralph said, "If I can rent it, it's a rustic little cottage in the country. If I can't rent it, it's a cowshed."

Ralph never held grudges. Hearn says he once explained that it was because "there's no tellin' when you might need that man's vote."

He told friends that he never voted against judges or the welfare department because "eventually, one or the other is going to get me."

Ralph also found time throughout his life to help his alma mater. Otis Lackey says.

WHAT HE DID FOR North Carolina State University is unbelievable. He is really responsible for the Department of Food Science. And he did things for the athletic program and other things that you wouldn't have thought he had any interest in. No

one could overemphasize what he has done for
that university.

Nothing could temper his generous nature. Ruth
Albright, his secretary at the dairy, says:

WHEN YOU HAVE A BOSS like Senator Scott, there
are so many good things to be said.

He has so much concern and compassion for his
fellowman. He listens to the people's problems —
and there are many — and then he takes time and
makes the effort to help in any way he can. He
enjoys helping people.

I have learned a lot from him. His philosophy of
life is fantastic. He never seems to get upset or
angry. His outlook is always positive, pleasant, and
humorous.

His bookkeeper at the dairy, Nell Isley, says:

THERE'S NO TELLING HOW MANY people he has
helped, people he signed notes for and many a
time he never got his money back. He has gone
out of his way for so many people and never
wanted any publicity for it. He always put the
other person first.

His wife was the same. Dr. Bill Roberts says:

MISS HAZELEENE WAS ONE of the finest women
you'd ever meet anywhere. She was always very

even. If ever Ralph got too excited about something, she'd say, "Now Ralph, you calm down a little bit."

They were a real team. She was always right there supporting him in everything he did.

V

THE KRONBERGS REMEMBER

There is probably no better single example of the philosophy that has always motivated Ralph and the people of Hawfields than the story of Rudolf and Katrina Kronbergs.

The Kronbergs were born in Latvia. For them, the end of World War II was the beginning of a long stay in a German camp. Mrs. Kronbergs remembers:

WE WERE IN THE CAMP for four years. We had nothing. No work, no place to go. Other people were going everywhere, to Brazil, to Australia, to London, England. We had a little baby and we thought, "Who is going to take us? Nobody." We didn't know what was going to happen to us.

And then one day, they came and told us that we must go to the office in the camp and there they said that we would go to America. We couldn't believe it but they said yes, we were going to America.

They were going as part of a Lutheran Church program. Some time before that, Ralph had contacted the Lutheran Church and said that he wanted to sponsor a family from one of the German camps. The Kronbergs, with their two sons and infant daughter, were selected. The year was 1949, just before Christmas. Mrs. Kronbergs says:

WE CAME FIRST TO New York. We flew because we had a little baby. If you had a little baby under six months of age, you could fly. No need to go in a ship.

A Lutheran preacher from New York met us. He talked real good German. He said, "There is no need to worry. You have a place to go. You have a home." He gave us breakfast in a restaurant and put us in a train for Burlington.

We knew not a word of English. Not a single word. So we don't know what is happening or where we are going. There was Rudolf and me and the children, a boy seven and one that was five and our little girl just six months old. When we got to Burlington, there was this big man standing outside the train at the station.

It was Melvin Hearn, whom Ralph had asked to meet the Kronbergs. Hearn remembers that morning as if it were yesterday:

IT WAS SIX O'CLOCK. I picked them all up and we went to Ralph's house for breakfast. And what a good breakfast that was. Mrs. Scott had fixed everything you could think of. The Kronbergs had been very limited in what foods they could get in the camp. No coffee or sugar or butter. And Mrs. Scott had everything on that breakfast table.

Mrs. Kronbergs remembers her first sensation was one of fright, not knowing what was really going to happen to them. She didn't know whether to eat or not, but her husband didn't have that problem. "He just kept putting spoon after spoon of sugar in his coffee," she remembers.

After breakfast, Hearn and the Scotts took the Kronbergs to their new home. It was across the road from Ralph's house.

Hearn recalls:

> THEY HAD PUT THE BASICS in the house but they needed food. So Ralph went on to the office, and Miss Hazeleene and Rudolf and their two sons went with me to the A & P store there. We'd go up and down the rows. I didn't know any of their language and they didn't know mine but we got to where we could communicate pretty good. We'd look at the pictures on the cans and packages and in that way we got enough groceries for a week or so. I went shopping with them for groceries several times after that.

While everyone else was at the A & P, Mrs. Kronbergs stayed in her new home. She remembers how bewildered she felt:

THE BABY WAS REAL SICK. I didn't have any diapers for her or food. I remember I sat there in the house where we live now and a relative of Mr. Scott's came over and we sat there in the room with the baby and I just kept wondering what was going on.

Later, I started learning English. There was no school for me to go to but from the radio and from meeting people, I started learning somehow. That first day, though, I just sit and look through the window. I don't know where I am or where I am going to be that night or what's going to happen. I didn't know if we were going to have a job or what we were going to do.

And then, right away, people start coming from the church and from the school. A group of young girls came from the school up there and brought us all kinds of presents. They brought us oranges and the children had never had an orange before. They have one and then they say, "Oh, I'll take another one. And another one."

People brought us food and clothes and everything. We were so upset that we couldn't sleep that night. That was because of what my nephew had told us. He came first to America and he would say in his letters that you have to be careful in America because sometimes salesmen come in and bring you stuff and then you have to pay. So when all these people kept bringing us stuff we were scared. We didn't have a penny in our pocket so we thought, "How can we pay for all this?" We didn't know it was all a gift.

We came here two weeks before Christmas, on December 14, 1949. One night soon after we got here, a whole bunch of people came out from the church and sang Christmas carols for us. They had gotten together at the church (we found out much later) and said, "Let's go and show them our love for them." And 90 or 100 people came to our house and brought bedsheets and pillow cases and coffee and sugar. Anything in the world you needed, they brought. We had no furniture yet. The room was empty and they just kept putting things in there and putting them in there. When they all left, we looked at all those things and we couldn't touch them. We just kept saying, "How are we going to pay for all that?" We worried all night about it and we couldn't sleep.

Then the next afternoon, a German lady came to see us. Mr. Scott had gotten her to come over and translate for us. She lived in Burlington and she came out about twice a week to find out how we were doing. So that next afternoon when she came and we told her how worried we were, she said, "No, all that is yours. You can eat the food and use the things and you don't have to pay for them. That's how people are up here. They just come and bring you presents because you are here and have nothing." That made us feel so good.

Then a couple of days later, a man came up there and two men were with him. I think to myself,

"That's not Mr. Hearn or Mr. Scott. Who are these strange people?" They come in the house and go around putting up curtains in every room. I think that after they finish putting up all those curtains, they are going to ask me for money, so I tried to tell them not to do that. But I can't speak English and they won't listen to me.

I just keep waving my hands at them and they just keep putting up curtains.

Then a long, long time later when I was working for Mr. Scott's son Henderson, I had my first paycheck and I went to Roses store one day to cash it. The girl says that she needs to ask somebody about whether or not she can cash it for me. So this man comes out and he says, "Oh my goodness, it's been a long time since I've seen you. You remember, I put your curtains up. I brought them over from the store and put them in your house and you were sure upset." He was real happy that we could finally talk!

That was our first house. And then Mr. and Mrs. Scott started building a new house across the road from where they were, and when they moved out of their old house, we moved in there. And that house belongs to us now.

Ralph also gave the Kronbergs jobs. Says Mr. Kronbergs:

I AM A FARMER. I had a farm back home. So I do the same work here. Those first five years passed very fast and Mr. Scott was so good to us. He treated us like family. We were that close. And the preacher, Mr. Buchanan, was so good to us. He came to breakfast that first morning we were here.

Mr. Kronbergs drove the tractor on Ralph's farm while Mrs. Kronbergs milked the cows. Their two sons helped and soon the family had saved enough money to buy a car. Says Mrs. Kronbergs:

MR. SCOTT LET US DO everything we wanted to do. He let us fix up the house and we put roses in the yard. He'd loan us his car whenever we wanted to go somewhere. I cannot find the words to say how good he was to us. At Christmas, he'd give us money and he even gave the children money.

When it came time for them to buy their own car, Hearn was the one who went with them to pick it out. He remembers:

RUDOLF HAD TALKED with Ralph about getting his own car. Ralph said he could arrange it and he went to the bank and arranged the loan for them. Then I took them to look at cars one day. I had the impression that Rudolf wanted to get the cheapest model, but he knew all about engines and he kept telling me that the cheap one wasn't built well. Said there was too much space between the engine and the side of the car. So he ended up buying the biggest and best Ford in the place. And he didn't need any money from the bank that Ralph had arranged for. Rudolf had saved up and he paid cash.

The Kronbergs' sons had a lot of adjustments to make in their new life, especially the younger one. Mrs. Kronbergs remembers:

OUR YOUNGEST SON WAS five years old, but in the old country you can go to school at the age of five. So I didn't know that I couldn't send him to school. The German lady who translated said that the school bus would come by the house to pick up children going to school. So it comes by and I put both of the boys in it. They go to school for two or three weeks. And every day, the youngest one brings home a little note. I think to myself that the teacher is just saying how nice he is, how well he's doing. I just think the best. And I save those little notes. And then after two or three weeks, the German lady came and she said, "How are the boys doing in school?"

I said, "They are doing good. I don't know about the oldest one, but the youngest one keeps bringing home a little note all the time saying how good he is."

She said, "Let me see the notes." And when I showed them to her, she said, "Oh my goodness, you're not supposed to send him to school because he's too young and every day, they ask you not to send him to school again."

So the next day, I don't send him and he cried because he can't go to school with the other boy and I cried because I'm not understanding anything that's going on here.

The Scotts would come by our house every Sunday afternoon. Mr. Scott would see me out hoeing the garden sometimes when he was on his way to Burlington and he'd stop by and we'd talk. When I'd be planting flowers, he'd say, "What are you planting those for? Plant something to eat!" But still, he loves flowers. He likes gardening too and he thinks everybody should have a garden.

The Kronbergs learned quickly about ways they could help the Scotts on the farm. Hearn remembers:

THE TWO OF THEM REALLY ran Mr. Scott's farm. Rudolf has a great mechanical aptitude. He knows how to fix tractors and all the things like that. He'd tell me what piece of equipment he'd need and I'd go get it at the shop in Burlington. And then in time he got to the place where he'd take the pickup truck and go over there himself.

The Kronbergs worked on the Scott farm for five years. And then Ralph told them that if they wanted to find another Latvian family who would like to work with them, he would let them have the farm. They wouldn't pay him anything the first year and then begin slowly paying for it the second year. But the Kronbergs decided not to accept.

Mrs. Kronbergs remembers that the week after that offer, some men came to the farm to work and they caused considerable damage to the silo. That night, she told her husband that it was too hard to find people who would work well without supervision. So they decided instead to put the money they had saved in a tree farm, and Mrs. Kronbergs went to work for Ralph's brother Jim who had a freezer locker:

> I WORKED ELEVEN YEARS for him, helping him cut and wrap meat. I had a good time there and everybody was so good to me and gave me steaks and sausage and other meat. Oh, they were good to me.
>
> The night before the first day I went to work there, I stayed up all night. I had gotten one of the packages of meat that was wrapped and I kept unwrapping it and wrapping it back until I knew exactly how to do it. Then the next morning, Jim and his wife said they were going to show me how to wrap meat, but I already knew.
>
> Rudolf had started working at the school and also at the church, sweeping them out. He used to work sometimes 16 hours a day. We both worked hard. We wanted to save our money. And so, when the children would want something like chocolate, we'd say no, maybe later. We made our own bread and planted a vegetable garden so we had all we needed to eat. All our children finished school and we put the oldest boy through college.

They joined the Hawfields Church and their daughter sang in the choir. They became much-loved members of the community that had welcomed them so warmly that cold December.

On the 36th anniversary of their arrival in America, Ralph and his children gave a party for the Kronbergs. There were presents and lots of good food for which Ralph's home is famous. But the most special aspect of that evening was the exchange of memories. The preacher talked about what the Kronbergs had meant to the community. Mrs. Kronbergs laughed about all the new things she had learned the hard way. She remembered the day soon after they arrived when she saw a package in the kitchen with the picture of a peach on it. Knowing that many of her American groceries had a picture of the product on the container, she assumed this was some kind of peach drink that was made by adding the powdery substance in the package to water. She stirred some up for the family only to find that the picture denoted the brand name rather than the product. She had stirred up a batch of Peach Snuff.

There were many people who helped the Kronbergs to make their new land their home. But most of all, Mrs. Kronbergs remembers all that Ralph and Hazeleene contributed:

SHE WAS THE NICEST LADY you ever knew. She was a perfect match for Mr. Scott. Both of them were so good to people. She was always saying to me, "I need to go take some pies to somebody. Come with me." Or "Let's go see this person because they are sick and we'll take them something."

So I'd hold the pies in my lap and we'd drive off down some country road to see somebody. She was always doing things for people.

And whenever somebody was sick in our family, there she would come across the road with soup or electric blankets or whatever we needed.

And the Scotts would take us out everywhere. They'd take us to Raleigh when he was there, take us to the legislature, take us out to eat. You cannot say enough about what they have done for us.

The love has clearly been from both sides, and the Hawfields Church cemetery holds a lasting monument to the bond between them. Ralph has marked out a place for Rudolf and Katrina Kronbergs beside him and their stone is already there, a permanent reminder of the lesson in Matthew 25:35 which says, "I was a stranger, and ye took me in."

VI

TERRY SANFORD REMEMBERS

Terry Sanford's memories of Ralph go back to Kerr's days as governor. Sanford was just out of law school and in the process of setting up his law practice in Fayetteville. He was also running for president of the state's Young Democrats. Although it was unusual for a governor to get involved in the race for that office, Kerr campaigned for Sanford's opponent Eugene Gordon. Sanford won, and he remembers his first meeting with Kerr after his victory:

THAT FALL, I WAS INVITED to a football game. Kerr was there so I went up and introduced myself — I had met him before. He said, "Oh, yes, I'm glad to see you. You know, it does a fella pretty good to get beat every now and then. I helped Gene Gordon because his brother was the only textile man in the state who helped me."

I took a liking to Kerr because of that conversation. He was cordial and not only that, he was laughing about the fact that he had tried to get somebody else elected.

Sanford saw Ralph from time to time during those years, "rather casually," he recalls:

RALPH WAS VERY MUCH for Frank Graham. He was running for the U.S. Senate during the time I was president of the Young Democrats. I remember Ralph was there and absolutely dedicated to that campaign. Ralph was always in that mold of being for things that dealt with people and their rights and opportunities.

Sanford and Ralph first became colleagues when Sanford was elected to the State Senate from Cumberland County in 1952, the year that William Umstead was elected governor.

THE FIRST LEGISLATION we really got associated together on was the Milk Commission bill. I supported it strongly. Of course, I didn't have any involvement in the milk business, but I thought it was a great piece of legislation to protect the milk supply and the farmer. And while *The Charlotte Observer* and others were complaining that it ran the price up for the consumer, in the long run it was designed to do just the opposite. So I had no problem supporting the bill, and Ralph and I began to get friendly during that time.

Education didn't get much of a shot in that administration. Nonetheless, we were both very concerned about education so that brought us together too.

At some point, I was going over to Greensboro and I said to Ralph, "I think Governor Scott ought to run for the Senate. He said, "Well, why don't you stop by Haw River and see him."

Ralph called Kerr and told him I was coming by on my way back from Greensboro. And I did go there and talk with him for awhile. That was the spring of 1953. By the spring of 1954, Kerr was running for the U.S. Senate and I was his campaign manager. So Ralph got me into that.

It was not an easy campaign. In 1952 Kerr had supported Judge Hubert Olive for the Democratic gubernatorial nomination. Olive lost and William Umstead won both the nomination and the election. Umstead never forgave Scott and the two men squared off again in the 1954 race for the U.S. Senate — Kerr's opponent was incumbent Alton Lennon who had been appointed to that seat by Umstead the year before on the death of Senator Willis Smith. Says Sanford:

NOBODY KNEW LENNON so it became a Scott vs. Umstead race. Governor Umstead just really emotionally despised Scott. He just had no use for him or *The News and Observer*. I remember once I went into Governor Umstead's office and, while I was waiting, I asked to see *The News and Observer* because they always listed where legislative meetings were going to be held and I needed to look one up. When I asked to see it, the staff person there said very firmly, "We don't have that newspaper in this office!"

I was on pretty good terms with all those people in those years but, of course, I was just a young squirt. Ralph was deeply involved in Kerr's Senate campaign and helped get up a good deal of the money. We ran that campaign on about $60,000. It was very hard to get money then. For one thing, people weren't accustomed to giving. If a person gave you $500, you'd think he had almost won the campaign for you.

Ralph got up money from various people. He worked the agricultural associations and State College alumni. Kerr was certainly the best friend that rural people or State College ever had in the governor's office. Nevertheless, some of them were opposed to him. A lot of them had fallen in with the Raleigh-type lobbyist and the old guard, so Kerr had some problems with some people. Ralph kept in touch with all of them and took a very active part in the campaign.

It was a successful campaign. Kerr went off to Washington and Ralph went back to Hawfields. Ralph had no chance of returning to the legislature for the next session because of a prearranged rotation agreement with Orange County. So he decided to run against popular incumbent Carl Durham for Congress. Sanford recalls Ralph's attitude about his losing candidacy:

EVERYBODY TOLD HIM not to run. Carl Durham by that time had a very distinguished name. He was co-chairman of what was then called the Atomic Energy Joint Committee, so that every other year he presided over it. He was a highly regarded person in Durham and Chapel Hill which was the heart of that district at that time. It would have been all but impossible to beat him.

I remember telling Ralph afterwards, kidding, "You know nobody could beat Carl Durham. I tried to tell you my opinion on that."

And Ralph said, "Well, everybody told me not to run so I just figured to hell with 'em! I'd run and show' em."

Sanford remembers the next political event that brought him together with Ralph:

IN 1956 LUTHER HODGES was running for election to a full term as governor. He had taken over when Umstead died in office in 1954. There was a little mini-conspiracy to run Henry Jordan against Hodges. Of course, by that time, Henry and his brother Everett had sort of turned on Kerr Scott. Scott had made Everett chairman of the party, but then Everett fell in with the old guard that never did accept Scott. Once or twice, he tried to cross Scott up, kept him from being the chairman of the delegation to the national convention, and by and large, turned out to be more of an enemy than a friend for most of the time Scott was governor.

But Ralph called me and asked me if I'd come up to his house. So I did. And there was Everett Jordan, Henry Jordan, Ralph, Kerr, and me. And they said, "We want to run Henry for governor."

I asked Everett, "Why are you all of a sudden on our side?"

And he said, "Well, you know, we never really did fall out." By that time, remember, Kerr was in the Senate. Everett was particularly anxious not to offend anybody and he certainly didn't want to fall out with a senator.

So I said, "All right, I'll help him."

I took Henry around to different places in the state where I knew people. And that made Luther Hodges mad. He called me up one morning and said he wanted to see me. He said he was going through Fayetteville so I met him at the Howard Johnson restaurant there. And he said, "Why are you against me?"

I said, "Well, I'm not against you. I'm sort of obligated to Henry Jordan and if he's going to run, I'm obligated to be for him. So is Everett."

Now Everett and Luther owned some Howard Johnson restaurants together. Anyway, the upshot was that a deal was made with Everett, and Henry withdrew, and Hodges stayed mad at me throughout his term of office. In fact, he supported my opponent when I ran for governor.

So Henry didn't get anything out of it and I didn't get anything but grief. I later chided Ralph for getting me into that trap, but he had gotten sucked in just like I was.

That was part of the reason for Ralph not getting along very well with Hodges while he was governor. Sanford believes that it was also due to Hodges' political style.

HODGES WAS A VERY difficult man unless you wanted to be his stooge. If you did, he warmly embraced you.

Ralph later said of him, "When you were no longer worth something to Hodges, he dropped you. He didn't know what loyalty was."

The division between Ralph and Hodges became more evident in 1958 when Kerr suddenly died (it was the fourth time in twelve years that the holder of that Senate seat had died in office). Many people thought that Ralph should be appointed to fill out his brother's term. But Governor Hodges would not hear of it and, ironically, appointed Everett Jordan.

What may have been a great disappointment for Ralph became a blessing to millions of North Carolinians. Ralph returned to the state legislature and began a 20-year period of service that resulted in vast improvements in the state's human resource, education, and agriculture programs. It began, Sanford remembers, with the campaign of 1960:

WHEN I RAN FOR GOVERNOR in 1960, Ralph was very involved in my campaign and very helpful.

He helped organize Alamance County. That was when he was running for the Senate. He never got beat in those years although he did win by some narrow margins. That's a fairly Republican county and always has been. And Ralph was always controversial because he always did what he thought he ought to do.

When I became governor, Ralph was always right in there helping me. There had been a long-standing tradition in the Appropriations Committee to vote on all the small things first and leave the big ones like education for the last. My contention was that, if you do that, you are never going to get the budget where you want it because you're going to say, "Well, we don't have the money."

I wanted to make them vote on education first. So Ralph and I got together and put up the motion and we carried it.

Ralph was involved in all the education programs during my administration. The big thing was to get the enrichment program enacted. That cost about $100 million which was a lot of money then. Ralph was very helpful. He supported the program and what was of greater importance when it comes to courage, he stood up to help get the money. Nobody wants to vote for taxes and it was great to have him there when we had to raise them.

Sanford and Ralph made a good team for education. As a result of their joint efforts, teachers' salaries were increased, additional personnel were hired by the school system, three of the state's two-year colleges became state-supported four-year institutions, the School of the Arts was established, and many other innovative, quality education programs were started.

The achievements in services for the mentally retarded during Sanford's administration were monumental. The path of those achievements all led back to Ralph who championed the cause of the developmentally disabled with characteristic intensity. Sanford says:

I REMEMBER RALPH'S GREAT interest in retarded children. It came out of his association with a restaurant owner named Emil Cortes. He had a granddaughter who was retarded, so Ralph brought him to see me. That was already a field in which I had promised to do some things because I was very interested in it. We really didn't have any special programs for mentally retarded children and I wanted to change that. But I didn't really know how and neither did anybody else. So in the interim between the 1961 and 1963 legislative sessions, we did a very thorough study. Ralph took part in it. Then we came with a package in the 1963 General Assembly which was one of the most comprehensive packages for mentally retarded children in the country at that time. And it was Ralph's leadership that got it going.

Part of the package that came out of the governor's study commission recommended the establishment of a

Council on Mental Retardation. Dr. Harrie Chamberlin was a longtime member of the council. Chamberlin recalls:

TERRY SANFORD THOUGHT so much of Ralph Scott and felt this was such an important area that he asked Ralph to chair the council. The work of that group brought North Carolina way ahead of most other states in education and services for the mentally retarded. Later, as the result of a push from the federal government, mental retardation expanded into the area of developmental disability, and the name of the Council on Mental Retardation was changed to the Council on Developmental Disabilities.

I chaired the council's Medical Committee. In 1963 and 1964 there was a push pretty much around the country to set up screening programs for infants right after birth to discover whether they were carrying certain metabolic diseases, particularly the disease phenylketonuria, known as PKU. The techniques for doing this had just been developed and the federal government had studied it and felt it was feasible to do it on a statewide basis.

A committee was set up to consider it and make a recommendation to the council which, in turn, would pass it on to the appropriate state officials to try to get funding for it. As chairman of the Medical Committee, I presented the recommendation to the full council at a meeting in Raleigh. I gave the council all the details and said we figured it would cost $80,000 to set it up and run it for the first year.

After the meeting, Ralph Scott came up to me and asked if he could have a copy of my presentation. He said, "I have a meeting with Governor Sanford at two o'clock this afternoon and I would like to present this to him."

I had just spoken extemporaneously, so I rushed around and found a typist and got it typed up. Then I tore over to the governor's office and met Ralph Scott outside the door and gave it to him. He went into his meeting with Terry Sanford and I went back to Chapel Hill.

The next morning, before eight o'clock, I was getting ready to go to the hospital to work and my wife was expecting a call from her tennis partner. So when the phone rang, she picked it up and said, very brightly, "Hi!" Then suddenly I saw her expression change. She quickly handed me the phone and whispered with amazement, "It's Senator Ralph Scott."

At that point I didn't know him as well as I do now — it was a rather formal relationship then. When I picked up the phone, he said, "Dr. Chamberlin, we've got your $80,000 for you."

Recounting the story nearly 25 years later, Chamberlin still expresses amazement at Ralph's ability to move so quickly amid the power structure of state government and accomplish so much. Ralph's meeting with Governor

Sanford was soon followed by legislative approval for funds to establish North Carolina's PKU screening program. The program grew into one of the most successful in the country with every hospital in the state participating voluntarily and an estimated 98 percent of all newborns being tested for PKU and other disorders.

Ralph continued throughout his career to make tremendous contributions in the areas of services for the mentally retarded and public understanding of the disability. In 1982 Sanford wrote a letter to the National Association of Developmental Disabilities Council regarding a proposal to honor Ralph for his work in this field. The letter said in part:

> RALPH SCOTT HAS DONE MORE, and has pursued the cause of the disabled for a longer time than any individual I know. When the Legislature insisted there was not enough money for the disabled, Ralph Scott has insisted that means be found. Ralph Scott has for over thirty years championed the rights of these poeple who, in many cases, could not help themselves.
>
> Early in my administration as Governor of the State, I appointed Senator Scott Chairman of the State Commission on Mental Retardation, which subsequently became the North Carolina [Council on Developmental Disabilities]. I knew he was the best man to be found, and I was right.
>
> His vision is not limited to the cause of the disabled. He clearly sees that this is one part of the larger picture, that these issues affect and are

affected by all the circumstances and events surrounding [them]. Ralph Scott is not a single issue
man. He is a man of wisdom and insight who will
not permit this cause to be put on a back burner.

His wit and persistence are legendary. His leadership in getting things done in government, in
medical care, and in life has been remarkable. He
was among the first to push for preventive medi-
cine. You will have before you a list of his many
accomplishments, and I will not attempt to enum-
erate them. I will only say that Ralph Scott is a
great man, and has served long and well, and is
truly deserving of recognition. . . .

Another letter supporting that proposed national recognition came from Dr. Sarah Morrow, then the Secretary of
the North Carolina Department of Human Resources. Dr.
Morrow had previously been the Director of the Guilford
County Health Department. Referring to those earlier days,
she wrote:

I'LL NEVER FORGET how I came to know Senator
Scott. While working for the Guilford County
Health Department, before the days of special
education programs, I found several mentally retarded children through a screening program. In
his home county, I met with Senator Scott to
discuss the urgent need for special education
programs. As a result, Senator Scott secured legislative support and funding for two programs — a
major step forward for North Carolina.

Under Senator Scott's leadership, the Council: (1) pioneered the implementation of a statewide screening program for phenylketonuria, (2) assisted in the establishment of North Carolina's first genetics counseling center, (3) endorsed and supported legislation for mandatory licensing of day care centers, (4) assisted in the development of legislation authorizing grant-in-aid subsidies to sheltered workshops and day care programs, (5) assisted in the provision of educational programs to developmentally disabled persons, (6) established five case management programs, and (7) expanded an innovative alpha-fetoprotein serum screening project.

Through our years of association, I have gained increasing respect for the accomplishments of Ralph Scott. He has provided real leadership in helping North Carolina deal with the needs of the developmentally disabled. He has earned the highest praises and acknowledgements our State can give. . . .

During Sanford's term as governor, he and Ralph joined forces on other statewide issues. Sanford recalls:

I THOUGH WE HAD TO START diversifying our agriculture. We were under all kinds of attacks from the Surgeon General on tobacco — the first Surgeon General's report came out while I was governor and it fell to me to defend the tobacco industry. Diversification of our agriculture was something I had thought we ought to promote but how do you get it moving? We had a food science area at State College, but it didn't get much support. So I said to Ralph, "Why don't we build them a building?"

Ralph said, "Well, it's not in the budget."

I said, "Well, put it in the budget."

Then I told him that we should go out there and announce that we're doing this. So we had an artist to draw up a picture of a new building and we went out there to a place on the State College campus and we stuck that drawing up on an easel and had a press conference and said, "We're going to build a food science building."

The publicity assured approval of the budget item for the building, and the building assured the establishment of a new Department of Food Science in the School of Agriculture at State College. It was a dream made reality for people like Dr. Bill Roberts, professor of the Dairy Department there. Dr. Roberts remembers:

IN THE EARLY '60s, WE WERE looking very hard at how we could process North Carolina food products here instead of sending them out of the state to be processed and then brought back here to sell. How could we get food processing plants, get that work for our people, and handle all our own products? Dean James of the School of Agriculture said, "If we can get an appropriation from the legislature, I'm going to set up a food processing department."

And that's what the food science building fund did. It provided not only for the building but for the teaching, research, extension work, and promotion of food processing plants in North Carolina. Ralph Scott and Terry Sanford did that.

Sanford remembers Ralph's interest in many other issues too, not all of them bearing the statewide impact of a food processing industry. Sanford says:

RALPH WAS ALWAYS ON THE SIDE of almost all good causes, whatever they were. He was not a provincial representative at all. But he certainly took care of his local constituents enough so that he got re-elected. And he was constantly coming to me trying to get me to build another road in Alamance County.

In 1964, as Sanford's administration was in its final year, Ralph scribbled a handwritten note to the governor which said:

Terry,

I talked with Ben about a short road which is .7 of a mile which I would appreciate it if you could allocate funds for it.

Thanks for the other.

Ralph

Sanford sent the note back to Ralph with a handwritten reply:

You have got all there was.

T.S.

Ralph became famous through the years for his efforts to get paroles for Alamance County natives in jail for non-violent crimes. Sanford remembers:

RALPH WAS CONSTANTLY COMING up to the office and saying, "Oh, these boys just did some little something and you need to get them a parole." And it would turn out that they probably stole a whole truckload of tires or something much more serious than Ralph said. His constituents could really not do any harm in his eyes.

When it was announced that President Kennedy had a back problem and his doctor prescribed a rocking chair, his chair was built in Asheboro, North Carolina. So I gave every governor in the country a Kennedy rocker, and I had one for my office. Ralph loved coming in and sitting down in it. He was always doing one of two things. He was either asking for something or giving me advice —solicited or unsolicited. One day, he was sitting there giving me some unsolicited advice about something I had done wrong. And I said, "Ralph, why don't you come over here every morning. Just sit in that chair, and before I ever do anything, I'll get your instructions on how to do it."

A broad grin spreads across Sanford's face as he recalls Ralph's reply:

"OH, NO," HE SAID in that gruff way of his. "I'd rather come over here and raise hell about it after you've done it."

VII

Two Staffers Remember

Joel Fleishman and Tom Lambeth were two of Governor Sanford's staff members who became particularly close to Ralph. As the years passed and each went on to new challenges (Fleishman to the position of Vice President of Duke University and Lambeth to the Z. Smith Reynolds Foundation as Executive Director), the friendship of the three men grew. Remembering their early association with Ralph, Fleishman and Lambeth recalled those years when North Carolina politics were sailing through some turbulent seas.

TOM: I came to know Ralph first when I was working as a volunteer in Kerr's Senate campaign. A group of us had gone over to the Carolina Hotel in Raleigh — where City Hall is now — where Ralph always stayed. The headquarters were in the hotel, but there was this little house at the side of the hotel, in a back room, where we were stuffing envelopes, and Ralph was there briefly that afternoon.

JOEL: That was almost certainly the first time I met him too.

TOM: I remember knowing who he was and having some image of him as sort of a rural political boss. He turned out to be much more human than I thought.

JOEL: Tom was a very idealistic young student at the time. A sophomore in college. I was older — a junior — and much wiser!

TOM: My next association with Ralph was during Terry Sanford's campaign in 1960. I was his aide beginning in November 1959. There were several keys in the state and Ralph was one of those as was Bob Scott. I saw Ralph constantly during the campaign. He was very much a grass roots politician and certainly a strategist and a good one. Very good.

One of the keys to Ralph's political success and one of the admirable things about him is that he never gives up on anybody as a potential supporter. He may once in awhile say, "Well, forget about him." But Ralph always tended to believe that someone who is the most distant from you ideologically can become your supporter if you just work on him.

Ralph even had a contact in the KKK. None of this ever required any compromise on the part of his own beliefs. He just thought that if there were people who had complaints, you went and listened to them and reasoned with them. It was characteristic of him to hardly ever give up on anybody.

Terry's campaign was difficult in the sense of the stress associated with it. Race became very much an issue. Terry ran against I. Beverly Lake. It was in the wake of the desegregation issue and the school desegregation decision and Lake was determined to capitalize on the views of the North Carolinians who were worried about racial desegregation in the schools. He made that the key issue of the campaign. The outcome with Terry winning was in many ways a judgment by the people of North Carolina that they were not going to be like other states in their response to racial fears. It was a watershed election in North Carolina that decided we were not going to do that. Terry was the candidate of moderation. Lake was the candidate of racial discrimination. Ralph played a key role in that election along with other people.

Ralph's approach to race was that it wasn't a matter of desegregation but of historic neighbors getting along. It went back to that time when he was little and the black man in the Hawfields community cast the deciding vote for the school proposal.

Ralph had a very good relationship with blacks as he did with the white leadership who were much more conservative than him. I think that was because there was a sense that he was fair. I think the reason he got votes in Alamance County from a lot of people who did not vote for the candidates he supported was that feeling that he would listen. A lot of people are willing to tolerate your disagreement with them on an issue if they believe you at least will pay them the courtesy of listening to them and respecting their views. Ralph was a master of creating that sense because he really does believe it. He is trustworthy.

Ralph never avoided supporting other candidates even at the risk of his own election. Office holders tend to do everything they can to avoid being identified with a certain candidate, but he always was willing to share his own political strength and popularity on behalf of others.

JOEL: Ralph made speeches for Terry's campaign. He was one of the General Assembly members who had the closest relationship with Terry. He frequently came to the governor's office after the election and had complete access to Terry.

TOM: He was there the day Terry took over and the day he left. There were not many people who stayed for the last few minutes of that administration. There was a new governor and people had gone off to court him. But Ralph was one who stayed to the end.

[During Terry's administration] I was his administrative assistant. I guarded the front door —

JOEL: And I guarded the back! That's the way our desks were set up in the governor's office. So when Tom wouldn't let Ralph in the front door, he'd always come around the back and poke his head in and we would start talking. And he'd say, "Is Terry in?"

I saw Ralph regularly and we worked together on a number of different issues. The one I remember most was the fight over the Speaker Ban Law. We were resolved to try to get that law repealed. Ralph volunteered to go out and speak about that to people. Ralph's constituency and his reputation gave him a particularly unique position from which to talk about it.

I remember particularly his speech to the American Legion. Tom and I helped write it. Ralph was very courageous about doing it because the source of support for that law was really the American Legion, the people who were very much concerned about fighting communism wherever they saw it.

It didn't matter who opposed something. If Ralph believed in it, he would speak out for it. He always said what he thought.

TOM: Joel handled the system of clearing people for all the appointments to boards and commissions and all the legal business associated with pardons and commutations. Ralph always had a lot of cases with him, more than anybody else, people who had been unjustly sentenced. And Ralph always had a candidate for everything, every opening on every board or commission.

The most famous case is the hub cap case. Only Ralph, Joel and I know all about it! I went back there one day and Joel said, "You know, Ralph was telling me about the worst case of an unfair sentence I have ever heard of. He said that there were several young men in Alamance County who have actually gotten an active prison sentence for stealing hub caps. It's unimaginable that any judge would put young people in prison for stealing hub caps and we've just got to do something about it. The judge obviously made a mistake. These are pretty good boys from nice families and they just stole hub caps."

Fortunately, Joel is a trained attorney, so he documented these things. It turned out that they had indeed stolen hub caps. They had also stolen the tires, the frames, the whole entire cars! When confronted with these facts, Ralph said that he simply had left out some of the details.

JOEL: I don't think I ever knew anyone who was more of an advocate in the interest of his constituents than Ralph Scott. I think it stemmed from the kind of politics Ralph believed in. He believed that a representative ought to represent his constituents and it's not up to him to make a judgment about whether they are right or not. He believed that the members of the General Assembly were there to advocate for their constituents and, in the case of the hub caps as an example, it was up to me to find out whether their claim had merit or not. Like a lawyer, you advocate and you let the people make the decision as to the justice of the situation. You don't prejudge. And without enough money to hire a lawyer to do that for you, the representative is the only avenue you have. Ralph believed that.

TOM: I can remember another person, a constituent of Ralph's, at a later time who had some wealth and influence and when he had some legal problems, I noted that Ralph never took his case. I think that was the difference to him. In this instance, you had the case of someone whom you could guarantee would have access to all the legal assistance he needed. But the people that Ralph advocated for by and large did not have the economic means to hire a legal advocate.

His interest in mental retardation is an example. There was clearly no political gain for him in that. He spent a lot of his political capital on people who were not going to be able to pay him back.

I remember years later, in the '70s, I went by and we had lunch at the Holiday Inn in Burlington and Ralph brought Emil Cortes over to the table and they recalled what Terry had done. Mental health was already on Terry's agenda because of John Umstead. He and his wife were very close to Terry. I remember driving John Umstead and Terry all across the state, visiting every one of the state mental hospitals. It was shattering sometimes.

Ralph's area was mental retardation and those children [who could be educated]. Ralph probably deserves the credit also for introducing into the whole mental health picture in North Carolina the new approaches we went on to take. He was always responsive to people who were looking for better ways.

JOEL: He was the leader in the Senate for the mental retardation bill. I worked closely with Ralph on that legislation and in shaping what Terry's speech on it would be.

TOM: Ralph was skilled at rounding up votes and at personalizing issues. He was very loyal to Terry and supported virtually all his recommendations.

Ralph also has a great loyalty to his family. And he was *the* General Assembly representative for N.C. State. The interesting thing is that over the years, he also became the representative for UNC-Chapel Hill. And he also became an honorary Tarheel.

And then there was the story about Ralph and Al Lowenstein, the nationally known civil rights activist who led demonstrations in Raleigh.

TOM: Al Lowenstein was periodically in North Carolina and then away for awhile. In the '60s, he was down here working on the faculty at N.C. State briefly when we were having civil rights demonstrations in Raleigh over public accommodations.

One of the most difficult things Terry had to deal with was the fact that this fellow from New York — although he had gotten his undergraduate degree from UNC-Chapel Hill — was down here fomenting trouble. The legislators weren't happy about it either.

Years later, there was a gathering here with Al and Ralph. In the course of the conversation, Ralph said, "Yes, there were a lot of legislators that were really upset about all that Al was doing about the civil rights demonstrations. And they were giving Terry a lot of trouble because they knew Al was a friend of Terry's. But I'll tell you what I did. I just told them all that Terry had Al over there among those students just making sure that everything was under control."

It was classic Ralph Scott. He could have gone and argued about freedom of speech, which he would have done if it had gotten to that. But he knew most of the legislators simply wanted to protest and be done with it. So he just said to them, "Well, Terry has everything under control."

I think Ralph knew that this would let some of the air out of Al too. I'm sure he thought, "Al, why did you do all that? We were doing all the right things to achieve those goals. Why did you have to give us trouble in the midst of it?"

Some of Ralph's success was knowing when it was important to take a stand on something and when you needed to handle it another way.

Joel and I saw a lot of Ralph in Raleigh. And then, Hazeleene would come down from time to time. She was always there when it was important to be there. She was obviously a great influence in his life. He loved her a lot. He was obviously crushed by her death.

His house is a monument to her. She made it into that wonderful home. We used to go up there for Sunday lunch, a big fried chicken lunch.

We never went to legislative parties back then. We were working hard. It's a different world today, more of the Washington sort of socializing and the staffs are larger. But there was always a summer lunch for the state government interns and Ralph would always come. One day, he brought Miss Mary [Kerr's wife] and Frank Graham.

Miss Mary was responsible for getting Kerr to appoint Frank Graham to the Senate. If you ever saw anyone who looked like the wind could blow them away but who was absolutely solid steel, it was Miss Mary. An extraordinary person. She was very fond of Frank Graham. When, years later, Frank's successful opponent appeared in front of her to shake hands with her, she refused. She said later, "No, I simply couldn't bring myself to do that." I remember once watching Miss Mary and Frank Graham sitting in front of the fireplace in her kitchen talking. I just sat to the side. And he thanked her and said she was responsible for his appointment. And she just said, very quietly and sweetly, "Well, I just looked over the list and it was clear to me that there was one on there who was better than everybody else so I just sort of said to Kerr, 'That's the one.'"

Ralph never lived in Kerr's shadow. He had his own personality and character.

JOEL: It took enormous practical wisdom and political art to keep getting elected in Alamance County. Ralph supported politicians who were in clear opposition to the majority sentiment in that county. And yet he continued to get elected.

TOM: His philosophy was that "The best world is to go this far. But we can only get this close to that point and I'll settle for that." And that's what any good politician does.

During the Sanford years, Joel Fleishman and Tom Lambeth were frequent visitors to the home of Anne Queen, the Executive Director of the Y at UNC-Chapel Hill. Her home was a popular meeting place for students as well as politicians and news correspondents. Ralph was also a frequent visitor because her home afforded him the opportunity to talk with students during the years when they were becoming a political force in the country. Anne Queen remembers those years well:

Ralph H. Scott

MY ASSOCIATION WITH RALPH was mostly with regard to the students during the turmoil of the '60s. He made it part of his business to get to know the students. They felt comfortable with him and he with them. It was a very rare relationship considering their radical philosophy. But he was always open to new ideas even if they were radical. For instance, he thought the scandal over Thomas Eagleton's psychiatric treatment was dreadful. He thought such treatment should be acceptable. He was always comfortable with ideas that were foreign to his generation.

All during the '60s, when there was an issue that involved attacks from conservatives, he always came to the university's defense. And he always tried to understand the students' side. He called me one night and said he was really concerned about the image the university was getting across the state, partly due to the student protests. He didn't want to stop their protests, but he did want the students to understand political realities. So I invited the president of the student body and some other students to my house and Ralph came. He spent three or four hours talking to them. He was never threatened by people with different ideas from his own.

His folksy manner helped him to accomplish a great deal. The students trusted him. He often dropped by the Y and would talk to whoever was there. He wanted to get to know young people.

He had great power as a member of the legislature and the Advisory Budget Commission and the Board of Trustees of UNC. But he always used his power for great good. And he served his constituents well because he really cared about them.

Hazeleene was also a wonderful person. She and Ralph had such a good relationship. I used to go up there to Sunday dinners with Joel and Tom. There was always good food and a wonderful atmosphere. They had a grand cook but the cook was off on Sundays, so Hazeleene did most of the cooking. She always had two or three meats. Always had fried chicken and most times a ham. Lots of vegetables. And stewed apples that she made that were so delicious. She was such a gracious hostess.

The Scotts have strong family ties and they support each other. Their family loyalty is so deep. I remember when Howard Lee was first elected mayor of Chapel Hill, he made some scathing comments about Robert. Ralph called Howard but he was out-of-town so Ralph told Mrs. Lee, "If your husband had known Robert the way I do, he would never have said those things."

Ralph and Howard went on to become friends. Ralph never closed the door to the opportunity for a good working relationship or to learn from someone or to teach.

Stilsie Reynolds served with Ralph for many years on the state's Council on Developmental Disabilities, which came out of Sanford's administration. She recalls:

Ralph H. Scott

THE FIRST TIME I MET Senator Scott was when my [retarded] son . . . was perhaps eight or ten years old. . . . Emil Cortes had a granddaughter in Greensboro a few years older than my son. Her mother had heard that I was actively working to promote classes for retarded children and called me to see if there was anything I could do to help her get her child in school. [Then] she asked me to meet with Emil. . . . He had already been talking to Senator Scott and he wanted me to meet with Senator Scott to explain it further. He made arrangements to bring Ralph to Greensboro to discuss it over lunch. . . .

The second time I met Ralph was in the lobby of the Carolina Hotel after Governor Sanford had been elected. . . . The N.C. Mental Health Association was meeting at the Sir Walter. Our group was staying at the Carolina where Senator Scott usually resided when the legislature was in session. We were in the lobby talking to Senator Scott. I related to him the story of a retarded child I had recently met and how elated [the child] was when something finally made sense to him. Ralph's eyes filled with tears and I knew that here was a man who genuinely cared about people.

He remarked to me [that day], "I want you to meet Hazeleene. She's swell!" I thought then what a wonderful compliment to pay one's wife.

As we walked over to the Sir Walter through the park, I explained to Senator Scott why I wanted a separate position in the new Department of Mental

Health for one person whose sole responsibility would be to work with programs for the mentally retarded. He said it so happened that he was having breakfast with the governor the next morning and that if Dr. Eugene Hargrove, who was to head up the new Department of Mental Health, had no objections, he would ask the governor and maybe include that recommendation in his address to the Mental Health Association the following day. . . . Dr. Hargrove was in the lobby of the Sir Walter at the time so I asked him if it would be agreeable with him. He was most enthusiastic. I related this to Senator Scott and he, in turn, asked the governor about it as promised. The following day . . . Governor Sanford made the recommendation. That is how the position of Deputy Director of Mental Retardation in the Department of Mental Health was established.

Later, after lunch, as we walked back through the park to the Carolina, Ralph was in a rare mood and he chuckled and remarked, "Now we're wheeling and dealing," which was the first time I'd heard that oft quoted saying [of his].

The Study Commission on Mental Retardation . . . having completed its report, formally presented it to Governor Sanford. For some reason, I was present and recall the governor's frankness. He said that he was most sympathetic with the plight of the mentally retarded but lacked specific knowledge and relied heavily on the recommendations of those most familiar with their needs, the parents and professionals who worked daily with retarded persons. He agreed to support legislation to establish a Council on Mental Retardation provided that Senator Scott accepted the chairmanship.

When [that council] was established, I am sure Senator Scott was responsible for my being one of the original appointees. . . .

From then on, as long as I remained on the council, I was constantly in close contact with Senator Scott. . . . He used to joke that when you lived within 30 miles of Emil Cortes and Miss Stilsie, you had to do something.

His office was always open to me. I spent many hours typing requests and explanations of projects we were working on. One of his first requests to me was that I not send him any handwritten letters.

He and Senator Tom White, with the backing of Governor Sanford and later Governor Scott and the fine cooperation of Bob Denny, Executive Director of the council, worked miracles.

Ralph Scott is a good man. Plain as an old shoe. Every time you needed him, he was always there. You could count on it. And he was always concerned about his constituents. He would stop anything to tend to the needs of the people who put him in office.

I loved his homespun humor, his total honesty, his understanding. He was always willing to listen but his level head knew there were limits. He knew how to get funds and where to grease the wheels, and without his many hours working in the legislature, all our dreams would still be just that, dreams. Without him, it's a different world out there today.

Hazeleene and Ralph

VIII

Bob and Jessie Rae Scott
Remember

Bob Scott's memories of his Uncle Ralph begin as a child. He and Ralph's son Henderson were about the same age, so his early recollections revolve around his cousin:

WE WERE IN AND OUT of each other's home all the time and we spent the night at each other's home too. As children we would alternate a lot. As the crow flies, our homes were about a mile and a half apart through the fields and we'd meet halfway. There was a huge ash tree there at the side of the road. We would call each other on the phone and say, "We'll meet at the ash tree."

We would play there a little bit and then decide which one's home we were going to play at the rest of the day. I remember we would say, "Well, what's your mama got to eat?" and that would decide where we would go.

Uncle Ralph was away at the dairy plant in Burlington during the day in those years and busy with his activities. So I don't remember seeing him a lot. His home was a warm, friendly, comfortable place. Maybe I thought so because it was kinfolks. But it was a happy home. And Hazeleene was really a special person. She was rather long suffering too with us children running around. When I think back about it, she was a partner to him in all that he did.

During World War II, when gasoline was short, Ralph and my dad and others who lived in our part of the community would walk to church on Sunday. My dad lived farther from the church than Ralph did, so my dad would start out walking and then Ralph would meet him at the road and then their brothers Jim and Henry, and Mr. Dewey Covington, who was a neighbor, would join them. There would be several of them who would walk to church, getting there in time for Sunday school. They would talk about their crops and they would gossip and talk politics, and by the time they got to church, they would have the world's problems pretty well settled.

One thing that impressed me about Ralph —and this was true of his brothers and sisters too —was their sense of humor. They all had a natural humor that wasn't contrived. Sometimes I think they didn't even realize they were being funny. It just came out that way.

Like the time when Ralph came home from the hospital after having his first stroke. Somebody said to him, "How did you get along?" And he said, "Well, all right, I reckon. They gave me all these tests. Even gave me a brain scan but they didn't find anything."

That's another thing about Ralph. He could always laugh at himself and see the humor in things.

I remember another time while my dad was governor. Ralph was in the dairy processing business but he had a small plant and he was competing against the giants like Sealtest and Pet. These big companies would undersell him to try and drive him out of business. So he introduced a bill to establish the Milk Commission, which would regulate prices. It was very controversial.

Apparently Ralph and my father were discussing it one Sunday morning as they walked to church. When they got there, they stopped the conversation and went on in. Ralph was evidently very upset with my dad for not supporting this legislation as strongly as he wanted him to. While they were sitting in church, Ralph kept thinking about it, and the more he thought about it, the madder he got. When the service was over and the benediction was pronounced, they all started out the door. They were sitting in different pews, so Ralph intercepted my dad going down the aisle and said, right there in church, "Dammit, Kerr, I need your help on that bill!"

They tell another story, and I know it's true because I was there. Like a lot of rural churches, in our church you had a place where you always sat. My dad sat in the pew in front of Ralph. I was just a little fella then. My feet wouldn't even touch the floor. I was sitting there on the bench and when it came time to take up the collection, my dad reached in his billfold and saw that he didn't have anything but a $5 bill. So he turned around and asked Ralph if he had any change. Ralph said, in a stage whisper that you could hear all over the place, "Aw, go ahead, Kerr, and put in the whole nickel."

Jessie Rae Osborne grew up in the nearby community of Swepsonville. The school there merged with the Hawfields school when she, Bob, and Henderson were in the third grade, so they became classmates. She didn't have much occasion to see Ralph in those early years. She says:

I CAME FROM A TOTALLY different background, growing up in a little mill village. But when Robert and I were married, Ralph and Hazeleene never had anything but acceptance of me, which made me know they were a totally democratic people. I always appreciated the fact that they were so accepting and supportive and encouraging of me. They were compassionate. And they were tough, very tough people when they had to be, when they were standing up for something they believed in.

They had great respect for a person who was willing to work hard to get what they wanted. If there was a young person in the community who had the potential but did not have the resources to go to college, Ralph made it possible for them to go. And he would never let anybody know it. Sometimes he would work it through the minister at the church. He would give the minister the money and then the minister would go to the parents and say, "The church has this money. . . ."

There is no telling how many people he touched directly. Not only children he sent to school, but there were families in the community that he made sure got food when they needed it. He would do anything he could to help people who needed it.

Bob has the same memories:

JESSIE RAE AND I WOULD BE over at his home on Sunday afternoons and you could never really get through an extended conversation with him because of the phone ringing and people calling him or coming by to talk with him. That was true when he was county commissioner and later when he was in the legislature. It probably never occurred to him to get an unlisted number. He just wouldn't do something like that. Nor would he go off somewhere so that he couldn't be reached. He made himself available. He never separated himself from people.

He would clip out articles from the newspaper and write a little note to the person the article was about and send it to them. It was always when a student had won an honor in school or when someone had received recognition or an award or done something commendable.

He really cared about people. He was people oriented. I think that was another trait of that generation of Scotts. They were populists. They believed in equality. Ralph did wonderful things to advance integration; he supported the ERA totally; and his work with the mentally handicapped, particularly the mentally retarded, is legendary.

Ralph's daughter Miriam remembers her father played a little golf for awhile and her mother was quite proud of his scores. But that was apparently the extent of his recreational activities. Bob says:

TO MY KNOWLEDGE, Ralph never had any hobbies. He didn't hunt or fish. He didn't collect stamps. He wasn't a collector of anything. He didn't go to the theatre or ballgames. He spent all his time on people.

He got to know some German prisoners during the second world war and he developed a personal feeling for them as he did for all people. They were prisoners of war who were encamped at Butner, known then as Camp Butner. The farmers in the surrounding area could get a detail of these prisoners to work on the farms. There was a labor shortage then. So my father and Ralph signed a contract with the government for that. I had the job of driving Ralph's truck down to Camp Butner in the morning to get a load of prisoners and bring them back up there and they'd work on the farm during the day. Then I'd take them back to Camp Butner in the evening.

These were older Germans, 45 or 50 years old. They weren't hard Nazis. These were people who had been drafted and they didn't want to fight the war anyway. All they wanted was for the war to be over so they could go home. They were quite gifted. They could fix anything. They would bring a violin with them or a harmonica and play German songs during the lunch hour. They were obviously homesick.

Bob says that Ralph was shaped by the family tradition in which he was raised and by the special little community in which he lived. He remembers the influence of the historic Hawfields church:

I SOMETIMES SAY THAT the reason we're Presbyterian is because there wasn't any other church to go to! But my father used to say — and I half believed it for a long time — that you didn't stand a chance of going to heaven unless you were a Democrat, a Presbyterian, and owned a Jersey cow. So I kept some Jersey cows around for awhile just to be sure.

The community was really the church and the school — the little Hawfields school where Ralph went and where I went my first grade. Those two places and the people in the community and his family were Ralph's world. And he had no desire to get away from the homeplace. When he built the dairy plant in Burlington, he didn't move to Burlington although a lot of successful business people would have moved to town.

And he never had a fancy office. That room that he ran the dairy out of wasn't as big as a minute. And he walked all the way up that flight of steps, those old metal steps. He never moved his office down on the first floor.

The rural world that shaped Ralph grew as he did. Says Bob:

AFTER WORLD WAR II, Hawfields began changing to a bedroom community. Now there is some light manufacturing. More people are around there now. It just tears us up, those of us who have been there all these years. We want to keep it like it was but we know that's not going to be.

Ralph made a comment one time when the county was talking about putting an airport out there. They wanted a larger airport because the local industries needed a runway long enough for their planes carrying freight to the West Coast. So they were thinking about relocating the airport and Hawfields was one of the sites. That was the only time my mother ever leaned on me when I was governor to try to influence me. She never did pressure me on anything else, but she got kind of upset about the talk of putting an airport out there in the community.

Anyway, the design they drew up had the runway in sight of Ralph's front porch and naturally a lot of folks went to Ralph and said, "Can't you kill this idea of putting an airport out here?" Now they were going to have to buy some of Ralph's land for this project, so he used to kid and say he planned to sit on his front porch and watch all those planes take off and count his money.

Needless to say, the Hawfields airport was never built. In 1965, Bob became lieutenant governor. He remembers:

I APPOINTED RALPH CHAIRMAN of the Finance Committee one time and chairman of Appropriations the next. This appointment made him a member of the Advisory Budget Commission and then, when I was governor, they elected him chairman of that group. It was really an unusual situation for Ralph to have been a senator under a governor who was his brother and then later under a lieutenant governor and then governor who was his nephew.

Another appointment I made as lieutenant governor was Tom White on Appropriations. They were a power. They talk today about how a few members of the legislature control it and control the budget process. Shoot, they don't know nothing! Ralph and Tom White in the Senate and a couple of members in the House ran the show.

I remember one day they gathered up at Ralph's home in Hawfields — it was a Sunday afternoon — and they wrote the state budget. They brought it back down to Raleigh on Monday, introduced it in the legislature on Monday night, and passed it that week. About six of them did that. They talk about how controlled it is now. It's a lot more open than it used to be.

Ralph was involved in budgetary matters more than anything else. He was chairman at one time or another while I was governor of both Finance and Appropriations, and those are the two most powerful committees in the Senate. That gave him a lot of leverage to work on other things and he was able to funnel money into programs for the mentally retarded and for education. Those were the two things he really believed in most strongly and he saw to it that money went for those programs.

He was a businessman himself and he certainly understood that it was necessary to make a profit. He understood the profit motive. He was a successful businessman, very successful, but he didn't have that conservative philosophy that a lot of business people have. He was always for the underdog, for those who were less fortunate.

When I became governor and Ralph was chairman of Appropriations, he already had a great deal of influence and he perhaps had even more being the uncle of the governor. He would come by the office to see how things were going or to talk with me about things. One morning, he came to the office to see me but I was meeting with somebody else, so my secretary said, "I'm sorry, Senator, but somebody's in there with him right now. I expect he's going to be tied up for a right good little bit."

Ralph turned to leave and said, "Well, you tell him he needs me a helluva lot more than I need him!"

And that was true. I did need him a lot more than he needed me. He was chairman of the committee and could pass legislation or not pass it.

Our relationship was always good politically and legislatively. He supported everything I asked for even though I think there were two or three things that he might have as soon I didn't propose, such as the tax on cigarettes which was highly controversial. But he supported everything I asked for and fought the good fight. He respected the office of governor and he understood how to use power to get things done.

Together, they did a great deal, and Bob's administration is remembered for vast highway expansion, free transportation for the handicapped, the beginning of a kindergarten system, high school vocational programs, and expansion of the community college and technical school system. The cigarette tax helped pay for many of the education programs and money was found for other achievements. But not without a quotable comment from Ralph. After Bob delivered his first legislative message to the General Assembly, there was some concern about how the new governor planned to pay for his proposed package. Ralph told the press, "He gave us plenty of thunder but the rain has to come yet."

The nephew and uncle joined forces on other issues as well. Bob recalls:

WHILE I WAS GOVERNOR, there was a strike of the cafeteria workers at the University of North Carolina at Chapel Hill. It was over wages and benefits. The workers were practically all black people. It so happened that the lady who was the head of the group was from Alamance County. Ralph knew her and knew her family. He was on the Advisory Budget Commission at that time. Things got real tense and the students over at Chapel Hill got involved. One thing led to another and the students took over a building.

Ralph was sort of the go-between, the negotiator. He could talk to me, being my uncle, and he had access to the governor's office. He also knew the people involved in the strike as well as the students and they had faith and confidence in him. So he became the negotiator, the pipeline.

He was walking across the campus one day and a student spotted him and said, "Senator, would you come in here because we're having a meeting and we would like for you to talk to us."

So Ralph went into the meeting and said to the students, "Now I know a lot of you all think the governor's a son-of-a-bitch. But I want to tell you something. There's a lot of folks that think you all are sons-of-bitches too."

Ralph helped to settle that volatile strike. Anne Queen, then Executive Director of the campus Y, remembers the day Ralph phoned her about it:

I HAD GOTTEN TO KNOW the black workers and black students well, and I had brought them all together with the faculty for talks on occasion. So Ralph kept in touch with me about the crisis.

One Sunday morning he called me and said, "Anne, I've just read the story in the Greensboro newspaper and if it's true, I think the workers are right." Then he asked me who was Mary Smith, the leader of the striking workers. I told him she was from Alamance County. He said, "If I had known that, I would have gotten her and Robert together before now. I'm sure my brother delivered her. I'll see Robert at church this morning and I'll tell him."

But it happened that Robert wasn't at church that day, so Ralph gave a note for him to Jessie Rae, and a meeting was arranged between the governor and the workers. Of course, a lot of people had been working to get a settlement. But this meeting that Ralph got scheduled was what led to the resolution of the strike.

There are other memories of his years as governor. Bob recalls:

THE ADVISORY BUDGET COMMMISSION is something of an executive committee of the legislature and they met once a month whether the legislature was in session or not. When Ralph was a member of the commission, he would come to Raleigh for those meetings and quite often, he'd be down there for other meetings too. He would come by my office on Monday on his way to a meeting, and he'd have a list in his hand, written on the back of an envelope, of things he wanted done. He wanted this person to get a parole. He wanted that person to get their road paved. He wanted somebody else appointed to some commission. He wanted a job for somebody's child. He'd have his shopping list. And he'd come by the governor's office and go over his list with me or Ben Roney or whoever he could get to talk to in the office. Then he'd go on to his meetings. And by the end of the week, he'd come back and want to know if we got it all done. And if not, he'd surely have it on his list again next week. He surely did work for his folks.

I said to him one time, "Uncle Ralph, the way you're going, when I leave office at the end of my term, there's not going to be a soul from Alamance

County in jail. And every road in the county will be paved." I told him that all the dirt daubers would have to leave Alamance County because there wouldn't be enough dirt road around to build a dirt daubers nest. They'd all have to go to Chatham County.

Bob traded wit with his uncle, to the delight of the press. A reporter came into Ralph's Senate office one day while he was on the phone. Ralph motioned to the reporter to wait a minute and whispered, "I'm talking to my nephew."

"The governor?" asked the reporter.

"Naw," Ralph replied. "This is my nephew who works for a living."

Ralph also liked to shrug off his critics with humor. Bob remembers one of the most famous incidences:

RALPH WAS AN OUTSPOKEN SUPPORTER of the ERA. When it came to the floor of the legislature, it was a close fight and it was getting right down to where it was going to pass or fail by only one or two votes. Ralph had been away from his office for awhile when a secretary who had been answering his phone came up to him and said, "Senator, I just don't know what I'm going to do. There's a man on the telephone in there and you wouldn't believe the names he's calling you. What must I tell him?"

Ralph said, "Just tell him the son-of-a-bitch ain't here."

Ralph believed in the power of reason, but there were times when reason wouldn't work. He recognized those times and always had an approach to bring the situation to an end. Jessie Rae recalls:

THERE WAS A MAN IN Alamance County who was worried to death about communists. He was absolutely paranoid about them and he was convinced that there was one behind every lightpole and under every bed, and he was sure they were going to take us over. He kept coming into Ralph's office talking about those communists, asking Ralph what he was going to do about those communists. One day, he came in there as always worrying about the communists and Ralph finally said to him, "I'll tell you what. You go home and get your gun and I'll go home and get mine and we'll just go out and shoot the sons-of-bitches."

After Ralph retired, Bob says he kept up on everything that was going on politically, and "of course, he continued to have an opinion on everything!" But he seemed to be content with what he had done with his life. Bob says:

I NEVER HEARD HIM TALK about wanting to be governor. He ran for Congress that one time and was defeated. He probably could have gotten elected if he had not run that particular year against Carl Durham. He was the incumbent congressman who had been there a long time and people liked him.

If Ralph had waited until Durham was out of office, he probably could have gone to Congress.

He didn't frantically campaign or work real hard at it. He took the attitude that "Folks know me and they know what I've done."

I never remember being involved in any fund-raisers for Ralph's campaigns. Of course, back then it didn't cost nearly so much. He probably paid for his own ads, for some posters and some radio announcements. That's about all you did back then. But he gave a great deal to the political campaigns of other people over the years.

Ralph's older brother, Dr. Floyd Scott, was a country doctor up in the northern end of the county. When the community up there put on a little celebration in recognition of Dr. Floyd's 50 years of service as a physician in the community, we all went up there. They had the service in the church. Somebody got up there and was kidding about all the politicians in the family. He said, "Dr. Floyd isn't like Ralph and Kerr and Bob and all the rest of them. When you see one of them coming, they either want your money or your vote or sometimes both."

Dr. Floyd used to say that he never could make any money because it kept him broke all the time financing the rest of the family's campaigns.

In 1982, when Ralph was nominated for a national award, Bob wrote a letter in support of that nomination. It said in part:

NOT ALL OF SENATOR SCOTT's contributions have been of a public nature. I have been in his home on numerous occasions at night or on Sunday afternoon when people would call him asking for his help on an individual problem. I have never known him not to take a phone call or to ask someone to call him back later or to call someone else. I have never known him to be too busy to listen. I have never known him to decline to offer whatever assistance or influence it was in his power to give. I know for a fact that he has always followed up on these matters, usually with success. This was done in spite of the demands on his time as an elected public official, a successful businessman and a church and community leader.

Jessie Rae says:

IN RALPH'S PERSONAL LIFE in the community as in his public life in politics, he always had time for people. He would listen to people who would come to him with their problems. He would listen even if there wasn't much he could do to help. He never turned anyone away.

He was absolutely the same publicly and privately. That's not true of a lot of public officials. He was genuine and people sensed that. There wasn't any pretense. Nothing hypocritical at all.

She says that she thinks of her uncle-in-law in only "the most superlative terms." The feeling is mutual. Family friend Betsy Warren Harrison says she believes that Ralph "admires Jessie Rae Scott about as much as anyone he knows. He sees her as having come from a background where she worked hard and going on to be a grand First Lady and a grand person."

Ralph's deep love for all his family made an impression on everyone who knew him. It was always a close family. Says Jessie Rae:

> IT'S A CLOSE FAMILY and yet strongly independent, each one of the family. And they are supportive of each other.

The family loyalty, the independence, the firm belief in education, the abiding faith, all those qualities were taught to Ralph as a young man. And then he grew up and became himself the teacher. Says Bob:

> THAT GENERATION — Ralph and his brothers and sisters — they all had certain characteristics and traits. They were real role models for me and others of my generation. I think it's right unfortunate that, in the period of time when my life was being shaped, I wasn't aware of them being role models. It makes me think how much influence they had on us and we didn't know it.

At a dinner honoring his family in 1981, Bob said:

> IF THERE IS ANYTHING that has been handed down to me and my generation from Ralph (or Uncle

Ralph as we know him and everyone else knows him), from my father, from my grandfather who died a month before I was born, I think it is two things.

One is a conscious sense of roots, of place and time, of community and of friends — all those intangibles that go together to make a strong bond of friendship along with an appreciation of church and community, and the characteristics that made them of their generation . . . what they were. . . . [These things are] the very fiber on which a society rests.

The other thing that perhaps they taught us can best be expressed . . . in the words of Theodore Roosevelt who once said, "It is not the critic who counts, not the man who points out how the strong man stumbled or whether the doer of deeds could have done better. The credit belongs to the man who is actually in the arena, whose face is marred with dust and sweat and blood, who strives, who errs and comes short again and again, who knows the great enthusiasms, the great devotions, and spends himself in a worthy cause and who, at best, if he wins, knows in the end the triumph of high achievement and who, at worst, if he fails, at least fails while daring greatly, so that his place shall never be among those cold and timid souls who know neither victory nor defeat."

IX

JIM HUNT REMEMBERS

The eighth and last governor under whom Ralph served as state senator was Jim Hunt. However, they had gotten to know each other long before Hunt's election to that office in 1976. They had first met when Kerr was governor.

The Hunt family were strong supporters of Kerr during his 1948 campaign. After his election, Kerr appointed Jim Hunt's mother to the state Board of Health, the first woman to serve on that body. It was one of a number of high level state positions to which Kerr appointed women, including a superior court judgeship to which he appointed Susie Sharp.

The Hunts were also involved with the Scott family in Grange activities. So when Jim Hunt became a student at North Carolina State College, he already knew one of the school's most active alumni — Ralph. They saw each other from time to time, but they first began to get well acquainted during the campaigns of Terry Sanford for governor in 1960 and Richardson Preyer for Congress in 1964. Even then, Hunt recalls, he didn't realize what a powerful legislator Ralph was:

Remembering a Champion

I JUST HAD THE IMPRESSION that he was a real plain-spoken country businessman-farmer who had a unique progressive streak in him. I did not know then what a champion of education and health and mental health and children and so forth that he had become. Status symbols didn't impress him. He sure didn't act like he was Mr. Somebody.

Awareness of Ralph's achievements came later, when Hunt was elected lieutenant governor in 1972, along with a Republican governor, Jim Holshouser. Hunt remembers:

THIS WAS MY FIRST legislature and it became clear to me that here was a wonderful champion of people who understood much better than most anybody else what North Carolina needed to be doing for its children and for its old people and for its sick and for all its people. He really needed to be in a position where he could have a tremendous impact on the programs. The best single way to do that is to be chairman of the Appropriations Committee because that's where the money comes from. So I asked Ralph Scott if he'd be willing to serve in that position.

Being chairman of Appropriations is a huge job because you have to master every detail of the budget. All the people who want things come to you. It is terribly time-consuming, and for somebody like Ralph, who is so tender-hearted and who cares about people so much, he would give them extra time. Some people kind of build in ways of holding folks off or cutting them short or not having to see or talk to them at all. But Ralph Scott isn't going to cut anybody short. He cares so much about them all that it was, of course, just an all-consuming job for him. But it was also a job in which he could have more impact than maybe anybody in the state other than the governor on what our programs were going to be and how much effort and opportunity we provided for people who needed our help. After we talked about it, he decided it was something that he would be interested in doing. And, of course, he just served in a marvelous way at a time when we made some of the greatest strides we've ever made.

I would say there are two major things that really stand out in my mind that Ralph gave personal leadership to. One was the establishment of kindergartens in North Carolina. A few had been put in on an experimental basis when Robert Scott was governor. But the full implementation came about when I was serving as lieutenant governor and Ralph was chairman of the Appropriations Committee. We phased them in so that, over a four-year period of time, we put kindergartens in every school in North Carolina. That was so typical and so appropriate because Ralph had so much concern for young people and wanted them to develop their full possibilities.

The other thing that stands out in my memory about his tenure as chairman of Appropriations is the fact that, although we had already been a progressive state with regard to mental health, we made some giant strides during this time.

The thrust was that here was a man who had been working and serving on these committees and commissions and giving volunteer leadership to human service programs. And then, as Appropriations chairman, he was put into a position to directly affect the budgets for these programs. And he made a tremendous impact when he got that chance.

And there was absolutely nothing in it for him. What was in it for him was the satisfaction of knowing that he was helping people who needed help, not just the disadvantaged but all of our people.

He was never just an Alamance County representative. He cared deeply about Alamance County, but I never saw him in all the years we worked together — and that was 12 years — I never saw him take a position on a public bill just because of how it affected Alamance County. He was probably the most public-spirited, North Carolina-oriented political leader I ever saw.

After I became governor, Ralph Scott was not always in the most important committee positions, but he was the moral leader for my programs in education and mental health. He was a person who could speak effectively to the moral dimensions of these programs.

And speak he did. During Hunt's two terms as governor, Ralph's leadership helped to win ratification of many important bills, ranging from more money to train teachers in science and mathematics to funds for sheltered workshops and a study of in-home services for the elderly. He was responsible for the establishment of the first state-supported group homes for emotionally troubled children in North Carolina and for major reform in the adult guardianship law. In the late 1960s, Ralph had begun trying to get officials of the University of North Carolina interested in a rehabilitation center for the physically disabled. During Hunt's administration, he obtained appropriations for the University to build and develop that center.

Hunt remembers other causes that Ralph also championed:

HE USED TO COME up to my office a lot. I'm sure he had a little more access to Bob Scott when he was governor, but not much more! Ralph wasn't one for setting up appointments. He would call Barbara Buchanan, my secretary who loved him just as much as I did, and he'd say, "Barbara, I need to see the Governor." And she'd say, "Well, Senator, come on up here at 5:00 or 5:30." Typically, he'd come at the end of the day when you had finished your appointments. He'd come at other times during the day too, and sometimes he wouldn't even call. He'd just come. And whenever he came, I saw him. I don't care who was waiting.

It might have to be a fairly short conversation, but I always saw Ralph whenever he came. That was because he always had a reason for coming and it was never anything to do with him. It always had to do with other people or with something in the legislature that needed to be done and with something to help me. He was a great political supporter of mine. When Bob and I had a primary against each other in 1980, I think it just tore Ralph apart.

That was a race between two longtime friends — Hunt, who was seeking a second term under a newly approved amendment to the state constitution, and Bob Scott, who was looking to return to the governor's office after an absence of eight years. But Hunt's popularity was so high that it would have been difficult for anyone to beat him. He won the primary and then the election with even more votes than he had gotten four years earlier.

Ralph took his nephew's defeat philosophically. Although he had, of course, supported Bob, he told a reporter that both men "are very capable people." He also said that it was a good thing for Bob to have run. "He gave the people a choice," Ralph told the press. "A lot of times it makes folks mad if they can't do nothing other than vote for one man."

So Hunt returned to Raleigh for another term as governor, and Ralph returned to his habit of visiting the governor's office. Hunt recalls:

THE ONLY TIME HE WOULD come for something for Alamance County was when somebody was in jail and he thought they ought to be parolled or their sentence ought to be reduced. And I knew exactly where that was coming from. Somebody's mama had been over to see Ralph and cried on his shoulder about her child. Ralph thought everybody in the world was good. He couldn't believe that anybody really ought to be locked up for long.

So he would come to see me and he would be just as persistent as if he were trying to establish a major highway or land a major industry for Alamance County. That one person who came to him with a tale of heartbreak or sadness just moved him.

I remember he came to my office one time, pleading for a boy that was in prison. He said, "Oh, he's a good boy. His mama has been to see me and he's a good boy. You ought to get him out of prison." You'd have thought from hearing Ralph that this fella was near to sainthood.

So I checked on this fella. He had one of the worst records you've ever seen. He had been in prison camps and violated all the rules. He had gotten into fights. He was one of the worst cases you could imagine. But Ralph had heard his mama's story and believed her just like he always believed the best in people. So he kept coming back to me about getting that boy out. I tried my best to explain why I couldn't do it. I showed him the records and talked to him and he just kept saying, "I declare, you ought to get him out."

Finally he said, "Well, at least get him closer to home. Get him moved to Alamance County where his mama can come to see him."

So while Ralph's story is one of major legislation and major programs for people, an equal part of the story is his concern about the human being, the one human being whom somebody brought to his attention. And that's a marvelous thing when a big, important, powerful person can get concerned about one human being who has needs, and be willing to listen and then go and be an advocate for that person.

I doubt that this boy's mama even voted for Ralph Scott. She probably wasn't even registered to vote and never had voted. She was nobody of any position in the community who could do something in return for Ralph. And here was Ralph Scott coming to see the governor about one single individual who was poor and powerless and whom some might think was unimportant. But they were all important to him.

Ralph was just moved by people and their plight and misfortune and needs. I really don't think I've ever seen anybody in politics who was more moved by human conditions than Ralph Scott.

And he was accessible to people. I often wondered how he got any work done because I know people had to have been at his doorstep or in his office just about every single minute. When you really care and respond to people, word gets around.

I never heard Ralph talk in religious terms although I have heard him pray. But if you knew your Bible, you could hear something that Ralph was saying as being straight out of the teachings of Jesus, specifically, the Beatitudes. Ralph lived his religion.

Over the years, Hunt came to know Hazeleene too, and his memories of her are filled with admiration:

SHE WAS A REAL MATCH for Ralph in terms of her love and her sweetness. No put-on whatsoever. I visited in their home many times. It reminded me of my granddaddy's home up in Pleasant Garden in Guilford County. Ralph's home was a very warm place where you were totally at ease. You didn't have to be anything but the way you naturally were. And his wife always had good things to eat!

Although I had been to Kerr Scott's home a lot, I never went to Ralph's until I was governor. Constituents were always calling him on the telephone. They'd get him up from the supper table and he'd leave the governor sitting there to go talk to them. That's the way it should be, but not many people would do that.

Hunt recalls that Ralph's legion of supporters and admirers did not include everyone in the state:

AS FOR POLITICAL ENEMIES, there were certainly a lot of special interest people who knew they couldn't get his vote and they certainly couldn't tell him what to do unless it was the best thing for North Carolina. Ralph Scott didn't see winning as everything. He felt that if some of the big special interests were going to jump on him because of the way he voted, let them do it. He was going to do what he thought was right, and he always did.

Ralph knew you couldn't make everybody happy, and he wasn't going to take on special interests. But he hated like the devil to leave somebody out of the budget who needed help. Yet you never have enough money. A lot of legislators have such obligations that they absolutely will not vote for certain taxes if it would affect their more powerful constituents, regardless of what the money would be used for. Their attitude is, "Well, you have to understand my district and my constituents and even though I'm normally a progressive person, I can't help on this one. You'll just have to spot me this one."

Ralph never said that. If it needed to be done, Ralph would stand right there and do the responsible thing, even if it cost him politically.

Ralph Scott never served as governor or lieutenant governor, but he couldn't have been more effective in either of those positions in terms of getting things done that he thought needed doing. The reason he was influential with those of us who did serve in those positions is that we believed in him and trusted him so much. If Ralph wanted it, it was probably the right thing to do, the necessary thing to do. And it was probably going to be oriented toward helping develop the human resources of our state.

State legislators, including those in North Carolina, tend to include an awful lot of people who are thinking about the short run economics of things. Ralph took the long view. He knew that in the long run, our state was going to prosper as we developed our people into the brightest, most productive citizens that they could be. Beyond that, he knew that our goodness would only be maximized if we helped take care of those who couldn't take care of themselves.

On the wall in Ralph's office, there is an autographed picture of Hunt as governor. The inscription reads, "To the man I admire among the most in this world, Ralph Scott!" That admiration came not only from Ralph's achievements but from the purpose behind those achievements. Hunt says:

I THINK RALPH HAD A VISION of North Carolina in which, yes, you wanted to get more jobs and more industry and you wanted people to prosper and so forth. He saw that side and was part of making it happen. But Ralph had a larger vision of the state, a vision that overarched the other one. It was a vision of a good state in which people treated each other in the way that God wants them to treat each other.

X

BILL FRIDAY REMEMBERS

Bill Friday first remembers hearing about Ralph in 1938 when he entered North Carolina State College. Friday was a member of the student government, so he often came in contact with Ralph, whom he says was "a volatile force in college activities."

After graduating from college, Friday went on to law school at the University of North Carolina at Chapel Hill and then, in 1948, a job at that university as Assistant Dean of Students. He ran into Ralph frequently in 1949. That was the year that U.S. Senator J. Melville Broughton, the former governor, died and Kerr, as governor, had to appoint a successor. He chose Frank Porter Graham, who was then president of the university and nationally known as one of the South's most liberal public figures.

Graham served out the remainder of Broughton's term. Then, in 1950, came what Friday calls "that notorious campaign" for the Senate between incumbent Graham and the conservative candidate Willis Smith. Graham received a plurality but not the required majority because votes were split among a total of four candidates. In the runoff, Smith won and assumed the Senate seat.

There were other occasions during those years when Friday and Ralph saw each other, occasions such as State College Alumni Association functions, Wolfpack Club activities, and meetings of the Agricultural Foundation. In 1956 Friday became president of the University of North Carolina and a new period in his friendship with Ralph began, a long and fruitful period during which the two men were fellow leaders in shaping the growth of North Carolina and the future of its citizens.

The political and educational events of the 1960s and 1970s brought them onto many a battlefield together. Friday saw Ralph in the midst of controversy, victory, and defeat. He remembers discovering through those events a unique and special man. Says Friday:

THESE ARE THE THINGS that made me feel Ralph was such a first-rate, decent human being:

First, Ralph was his own man. He kept his independence even while his brother was governor. Later, when his nephew became governor, he still kept his own ideas about things. And yet, there was an intense loyalty in the Scott family that made them respect each other's opinions and still pull together when there was something important to be done.

The Scotts are a great North Carolina family. They have been a positive influence in the state's political history, in Alamance County's growth and development, and in the Orange Presbytery history as well. Ralph grew up with that same sense of independence and individualism that had made so many members of his family leaders and bene- factors of our state.

Second, when Ralph told you what his judgment was and where he stood on an issue, you could rely on him. There was never any suggestions of dupli- city or deviousness or deception. He was always totally straightforward and totally open with you. That was true even sometimes when you got the feeling that later he might have preferred that the issue be handled in a different way, he still stuck to his word. He never wanted people to think that his word was not good.

The third thing about Ralph was that he worked hard to understand things. A lot of people shape opinions before they have really studied the subject. Not Ralph. He wanted to know the facts and he would work at learning so he could understand all sides of the situation. I spent a great deal of time over the years getting up facts for him. He wasn't satisfied until he understood an issue thoroughly.

A fourth fact about Ralph is that his interests have always been statewide. A lot of people would comment, for instance, that when it came to educa- tion, he was only a supporter of N.C. State. But the fact is that he was a strong supporter of other educational institutions in this state. He was a great supporter of the University of North Carolina at Chapel Hill, of developing the community college system and public television, and of expanding the university system throughout the state.

The fifth thing about Ralph is that he enjoyed a controversy. He'd stir up a ruckus when things got too quiet. He just enjoyed doing it and he'd do it in clever ways. He had great skill at coining phrases. He could say things that I expect he had thought about a good deal and was just waiting for a chance to say them. He was clever, very clever. And he always made a situation easier. As difficult and stressful as it might be, he would find some humor and lighten the load that might be bearing down on everyone.

A sixth element that shaped Ralph was that he dearly loved his family. His relationship with his wife was something quite beautiful to see. She was an enormous influence in his life. And I'm sure when she died, an enormous void was created in his existence. You can't live together that long and work together that long and be so much a part of each other's thinking and being and not feel a great sense of loss. But she had an awful lot to do with helping him shape his philosophy about things. She was really a good woman, a very good woman. And you enjoyed her company.

Seventh, Ralph kept on growing. He was always poking around trying to find new things, new ideas, new ways of doing things, better ways of doing them, cheaper ways of doing them. He maintained that kind of intellectual curiosity which makes people young.

An eighth characteristic about Ralph was that he did so many things that most people never knew about. He had a deep sensitivity and in a lot of ways, he is a very tender man. He did so much for mentally handicapped people, for people who had been terribly disadvantaged by bad breaks in their lives, and for people who had severe health problems. Ralph would find ways to make things easier and better for them.

When you're thrown with a man who has these kinds of characteristics, you encounter a great teacher. In his life and work, he taught everyone who knew him. We learned by observing how he did things. We learned by his tenacity. We learned by his intensity that was dramatic at times. We learned by his tenderness.

Ralph teaches that you don't do things with any sense of repayment or getting any award or recognition for achievement. You do it because it's important to do and you are blessed with the knowledge and understanding of seeing that. I'm sure that this has motivated him all of his life and has caused him to be such an inspiration to people.

Friday pauses only briefly in his recollections as he remembers another side of his special friend:

BUT RALPH COULD BE TOUGH and he could be harsh when he was fighting for what he believed in. If you were going to take on Ralph Scott, you had better know your lessons; he did. He was a real competitor. And he made the democratic process a lively one. He would say that if you had an idea that was better than his, prove it to him. He wouldn't change his mind until you did.

Whenever Ralph saw a problem, he went to work. An example was the speaker ban issue. Ralph understood that young people are better for having the opportunity to challenge ideas. That's what a university really is. Ralph saw that it had to be free, to talk, argue, debate, reconcile, compromise if you can, and go on.

Ralph had enormous faith in young people. He believed in their basic decency, rejoiced in their great energy. He would go to the student assemblies to be involved with young people. He'd talk with them about the budget and other political isues. No one believed in young people more than Ralph did.

In all of the issues he dealt with, Ralph was a stabilizer. He had a position but he never let anything get out of hand. When he saw that compromise was necessary, he'd be about it. He would compromise to get to the next step. That's the way the issue about building a medical school at East Carolina University was resolved. It was a long, long controversy and Ralph was the one individual who resolved it through the legislative process. He more than any other member of the General Assembly brought that decision to fruition. That was typical of him. He was always looking and watching and scanning.

When you're a strong type of personality like that, you inevitably make a few enemies. Now I've seen some people get angry with him and fuss and harangue. But a lot of that was envy. A lot of his critics were just saying that they wished they were more like him, that they were that independent, that they could be that forceful, that they could work and do things of the caliber and quality that he did. There is no doubt in my mind about that.

When you sit back and look at this family and see Kerr and Ralph and their sister Elizabeth Scott Carrington and Ralph's wife and Kerr's wife and Robert and Jessie Rae, it really is very reassuring. That's because this family recognized a role they could play in public service and each, in his own way, made that contribution. They were important contributions, very substantial contributions, both individually and as a group. And their impact on North Carolina from World War II to the present day is really unique. Few families have impacted the state the way they have.

Ralph used to laugh and say, "I've been governor twice. Why would I want to be governor again?" He was always kidding about his shadow role, as historians call it, which he played in both his brother's and his nephew's administrations. But he had all that he wanted to do. Ralph had enormous power and he used it thoughtfully and carefully.

Ralph is one of North Carolina's colorful characters of the post World War II era. There are not many like him on the scene and I don't know if there ever will be another. The events of the years immediately following a devastating war, the advent of the GI Bill, the complete turnaround of the American economy, the fact that this country was thrust into internationalism when most people didn't want it, the emergence of the racial issue, all these things and many, many more were whirling around our lives, and Ralph understood them. And he was a stabilizer while these issues were being debated and resolved. That is an invaluable quality for a public servant to possess. He deserves every accolade the state could give him. I think the state ought to acknowledge that kind of public service and that quality of public service because lots of times it's a very thankless experience. You keep going only because you believe it's right. That was Ralph's spirit.

Friday's recollections turn another corner in Ralph's multi-faceted character. He says:

ANOTHER GREAT THING about Ralph Scott is that he's fun. You enjoy being with this fellow. I always found him a great source of joy and humor and jokes. And you'd better watch out or he'd be telling a joke on you next! But that's all right too, because you knew that first, last, and always, Ralph was an abiding friend. That's a rare quality today.

We had a lot of fun together. He'd kid me about the guest box at the Carolina football stadium.

He'd say that he wanted to come over to "one of those ham and cracker parties," as he called them.

Ralph and I had a common failing — we loved to eat. We used to talk about fresh vegetables and cornbread and milk, about life on the farm, about hunting. Neither of us is a hunter. I'm sure that Ralph felt as I did, although he wouldn't tell you, that a deer was one of nature's great creations so he couldn't take a gun and kill it. That was the sensitivity in him that a lot of people don't see. But with children and animals and land and flowers and displaced people and handicapped people and mentally troubled people, his heart was as big as his farm. He had a place for everyone of these in his heart and his thinking. He was determined to do something for people who didn't have the ability to do for themselves. He was sort of a self-appointed vigilante in that sense. And to this day, Ralph is still like that.

Ralph experienced the depression years. He saw the price of deprivation. He understood what it meant for people to be poor and hungry and that memory never left him. The discipline of that hard work on the farm, the notion that work is important, that it is a powerful force in helping you to be a good citizen, those were lessons he learned as a boy that never left him.

In 1965 Ralph was made a member of the Order of the Golden Fleece at the University of North Carolina at Chapel Hill. It was the first time that anyone who was not an alumnus or faculty member had ever received that prestigious honor. The citation read in part:

RALPH HENDERSON SCOTT . . . ever ready to do battle for the cause of education, an outspoken friend of the University, partisan for the cause of the mentally retarded, a public man with a capacity for clarity, a conscience for justice, and the vision to see and to follow to the end of the row.

Friday sums up Ralph's achievements in much the same way. He says:

IF YOU WANT TO KNOW what Ralph's monument really is, just look around you. It's the universities. It's community colleges. It's farmland and children and the symphony. He was involved in all these things, in making good things happen.

And he did it without any thought of personal gain. That thought would never ever cross his mind. Not Ralph. He was a man of character and integrity.

Ralph had a role to play in society and he has done it in a way that gives him great personal satisfaction because he did his best. Not enough of us can say that. But his greatest achievement was that, by being the kind of person he was, he became a great teacher.

As he got older, like all of us, Ralph mellowed a good deal. He became retrospective. I'd go to see him and we'd talk. He'd look back and say, "Well, maybe we could have done this better or done that better."

I've never known a man who loves life more fully. He loves the land and animals and people. He believes in husbanding and utilizing every resource you have because it's a gift.

A lot of people don't know that Ralph was deeply influenced by his religion. His life has been his way of implementing the injunction in James 1:22: "Be ye doers of the word, and not hearers only. . . ."

Ralph has always been a doer. He'll still be doing his last day on earth because that's the spirit in him. He grew up in that Presbyterian tradition that teaches there are things to be done and, therefore, you must be about your work.

A doer of the Word. Recalling all that Ralph did for individuals as well as for North Carolina citizens, Friday says:

As I LOOK AROUND this state at the people I've known who were creative and achieved things, he would be on every list I would write. Ralph is one of the really noble people I have known.

XI

PERENNIAL MEMORIES

In June of 1977, as the General Assembly was coming to a close, Ralph had a heart attack. It slowed down his activity but not his wit. When a reporter asked him soon afterwards how he was doing, he said, "Hell must be as crowded as Central Prison 'cause I'm still here and doin' all right."

When he was feeling well enough to get out again, people were constantly coming up to him, asking how he felt and telling him that he looked good. That prompted him to comment to family friend Betsy Warren Harrison, "You know, there really are three ages of man — youth, middle age, and 'you sure are looking good.'"

Wishes for his speedy recovery poured in. Virginia Griggs, writing in her column for the local *City-County Newspaper*, said:

RALPH SCOTT WILL ALWAYS have friends. These friends are people such as [my husband] Jim and me and the many others that he has helped get started in different aspects of life. He always gives good advice and has a merry smile and a twinkle in his eye. He also has a wit and wisdom about him that is unforgettable.

That is why there are so many people wishing him a speedy recovery. This is not only because he is one of our country's and state's most significant human resources but because he is truly a gentleman. All of us are very proud that our paths have crossed with his.

In 1980 Ralph ran again for the legislature. This time he lost. It was only the second defeat of his long career and the first one in 24 years. Ruth Relos remembers asking him the next day how the election came out. "I got beat," he said, matter-of-factly. No bitterness. No remorse. The people had voted and that was that. Alamance County had continued to grow more conservative as new industry and new people moved into the once rural area.

Letters poured in from constituents, colleagues, and friends, with remarks about the election and about Ralph's career. Among them were these comments:

I KNOW IT MUST BE disappointing to have lost the election. However, I'm sure it was nothing personal. It just came at a time when people decided they wanted a change and never stopped to consider the consequences. As the old saying goes, "The grass always looks greener on the other side, until you get there."

Ralph H. Scott

THIS IS TERRIBLE NEWS, especially because of your vast knowledge of the state budget, your constant dedication to the mentally retarded citizens, and your exemplary leadership on their behalf. . . . I will never forget the day that the lieutenant governor and the speaker of the house said in their respective sessions that the guardianship bill was coming up for a vote, that Senator Scott had called from his hospital bed that morning to make sure that it was going to be voted on that day, and that Senator Scott wanted that bill passed. As you well know, the guardianship bill sailed through with nearly unanimous votes in both houses.

DURING 1972-76 . . . there were times it seemed State government might come to a halt except for your leadership in moderating differences so the needs of the people wouldn't suffer.

YOU GO OUT OF OFFICE in some mighty good company, and with your reputation as a Christian statesman and gentleman intact.

OVER THE PAST THREE DECADES you have been the single most influential person in the State, and you have been at the forefront of virtually every practical, progressive program. You should take great

---

pride in the length and quality of your career and the respect and affection you are accorded throughout North Carolina.

Ralph's old colleague Wade Barber wrote:

I DIDN'T LEARN UNTIL last night that Alamance seems to have gone all out Republican and that you were defeated. I am sorry. Probably the greater part of the time over the years, you and I have disagreed. However, we have always learned to disagree without being disagreeable. I have always admired your forthrightness — your readiness to speak your opinion.

Sam Ragan wrote from his desk at *The Pilot* newspaper to say:

I WAS SADDENED WHEN I heard of your defeat in Tuesday's election, but I know that it was not you but the State of North Carolina which was the loser.

Ralph seemed to accept the changing winds that had finally put a Republican in his Senate seat, but at a farewell gathering in his honor, the press reported that he was "visibly moved."

No wonder. Legislators and other politicians and friends stood up to pay him tribute. For three hours, they talked about his achievements and his honesty and strength and compassion. Howard Lee, who by then was Secretary of

Natural Resources and Community Development, called Ralph "one of the most gentle and finest men who ever walked in North Carolina." One representative said that because of his absence from the General Assembly "Alamance County is going to suffer. North Carolina is going to suffer." When the ceremony was over, a reporter asked Hazeleene for a comment. She said simply, "I'm glad he's going to be home."

In 55 years of marriage, Hazeleene had shared her husband with hundreds of people. Now at last it seemed she would have some time with him alone. It turned out to be less than a year. In 1981 Hazeleene died and her passing, wrote Russell Clay, "left a lonesome place against the sky."

Sometime later, when Ralph was talking with Ruth Relos about Hazeleene's death, Ruth asked him if people remember their loved ones the way they are just before their death or the way they used to be. Ralph said, "Just before they die, they are even more precious."

In the months that followed, Ralph stayed busy accepting the awards and commendations that one group after another bestowed on him. At one ceremony, D.J. Walker, Jr. said in his speech:

> HE HAS NOT RETIRED. Nevertheless, when people got the notion that he had, they began to vie with one another — statewide groups and local groups all over North Carolina — to honor and venerate him for his long service. It is a wonder that he has any humility left. I have participated in two or three of these dedications myself. But I can attest that he appreciates each one of them.

After one evening of tributes, Ralph got up and said, "I don't know about you folks but I've had about as much of this stuff as I can stand."

Each honor, each word of appreciation made a deep and heartfelt impact on this outwardly gruff, inwardly tender man. In 1985 the State Senate voted to declare a "Ralph Scott Day." Jim Hunt says that the legislators were "as unanimous about that as anything they had ever done."

The Senate declaration said in part:

RALPH SCOTT, TO A DEGREE unsurpassed by any citizen of this State, has been an unyielding advocate and friend of the mentally afflicted and physically disabled, devoting a lifetime of leadership and service to their cause . . . [he] values sincerity more than gold . . . we operate in the giant shadow of [this] man . . . .

At the luncheon in his honor on Ralph Scott Day, his old Senate colleagues reminisced about the qualities that made him, as Monk Harrington put it, "just a very lovable man." They remembered the question he'd always ask anybody who came by his office in the middle of the day: "Wanna go get a hotdog?"

And they remembered his earthy bluntness. One speaker told about a freshman senator who sat beside Ralph. Each time the man would go to stand up and say something, Ralph would pull on him and say, "Sit down, you damn fool, or you'll make a damn fool of yourself."

Lieutenant Governor Bob Jordan said that Ralph "isn't a senator — he's a legend."

A legend who left monuments behind. The state's community college system. Rural health facilities. Numerous buildings at North Carolina State University. The Department of Food Science at that university. Statewide kindergartens. The Milk Commission. The State Farmers Market in Raleigh. A research farm at N.C. State University. A $10 million expansion at North Carolina Memorial Hospital. The first genetics counseling center in the state. The PKU screening program. The School of Veterinary Medicine at N.C. State. The medical school at East Carolina University. The livestock building at the State Fairgrounds. Sheltered workshops, group homes, rehabilitation services, the Special Olympics, and countless other programs to help the developmentally disabled. And more.

Ralph also championed environmental issues long before it was fashionable. He championed the elderly long before they were viewed as a political force in this country. He once said:

I AM VERY CONCERNED about older people. It is tragic how some of them have to live. They reach old age and they aren't prepared for it financially or emotionally.

He was determined to do something about that so he sponsored a bill to give them a tax break and the bill became the Homestead Exemption Act of 1971. Many of his legislative colleagues say that this was Ralph's single most outstanding, lasting achievement, and the tax break it provides has been increased in years since then.

And then there were the individuals . . . the children he put through school, the parents he helped to find jobs, the helpless and powerless people to whom he lent his strength and his power.

Be ye doers of the Word, and not hearers only.

As a private citizen and later as a public servant, Ralph answered that Biblical charge. In a Senate career that spanned nearly thirty years and the administrations of eight governors, Ralph dedicated all that was in him to the citizens of his county and his state. He championed the poor, the elderly, and the mentally handicapped. He championed the cause of equal rights and better schools and integrity in government. He championed hope and won the battle for millions of North Carolinians.

Jim Graham says:

RALPH POSSESSED TWO great attributes — vision and determination. Blended with that dedicated strength and unbelievable generosity, he was absolute brilliance.

Betsy Warren Harrison says:

THERE IS A NORTH CAROLINA state flower, a state motto, a state bird. If there were a state treasure, it would surely be Ralph Scott.

A treasure whose energy and compassion became circles that took in everyone around him. "Anytime you were with him," Jim Graham remembers, "some of him would rub off on you." And that is his greatest legacy.

Ralph wanted life to be good. And he believed it would be good, if only those who were able would help those who were not. If only the strong would champion the weak. If only we all would be doers of the Word.

When Ralph Scott used to campaign for the General Assembly, back in the days when you went door-to-door instead of television studio-to-television studio, he would hand out a little flier with his name and a few words on it, and a little package of Forget-Me-Not seeds. What he never realized was that every act in his long and active life was one of those seeds. They were strewn throughout North Carolina in the hearts of hundreds of people who knew him and millions more who know only the results of his life's work. They remain perennial reminders of the champion who rode through North Carolina, a doer of the Word.